One-Legged Seagull

A Warrior's Journey to Inner Peace

JOEY AVNIEL

Copyright © 2011 Joey Avniel

All rights reserved.

ISBN: 0615521479
ISBN-13: 978-0615521473
Published by Barefoot Mind Inspiration

Editing: Jessie Marrero & Glenda Shenkal
Cover Designed by Sagi Meir

http://www.oneleggedseagull.com/

DEDICATION

I want to dedicate this book to all of you who are looking for your inner peace, and are brave enough to go through the journey to find it. I know how hard it is as I'm walking this path for over a decade. Be at peace.

CONTENTS

	Acknowledgments	i
	Introduction - can A Warrior find Peace?	iii
1	My Weakness Might Someday Become an Advantage	1
2	Three Pairs of Frantically Waving Arms	6
3	My Green Belt Story	12
4	It Takes Two Legs to Kick	19
5	Next Week is Always a Week from Now	25
6	What's Wrong with My Attitude?	31
7	The Genie Fell Asleep	38
8	The Win is Treasured in the Act of Surrendering	44
9	Every Nothing is Something	47
10	I Can Only Have Short Term Relationships with Drinks	60
11	Maybe What is Right for Me isn't Right for You	63
12	The Artist Sees the Angel Trapped in the Marble, and Carves it to Set Him Free	68
13	Even a Veteran Master Like Me Needs to be Reminded That He's the Creator of his Own Reality	74
14	You are as Good a Teacher as I am	81
15	You Can't Teach an Old Dog New Tricks	92

16	The Big Confrontation	94
17	Only in Movies Does the Hero Win the Battle Against Evil and Ride off into the Sunset	104
18	In Order to be a Great Artist, You Must be Willing to be An Awful Artist First	108
19	Why is it so Hard to Say I'm Sorry?	119
20	I Need to Find Someone Like Him as Well	131
21	Yesterday's Enemies	133
22	I Want to Hear a Story	145
23	What if Everything was Transparent?	150
24	It's a Jungle Out There, Not a School Playground	160
25	The Diary	163
26	In Okinawa, Belt Mean, "No Need Rope to Hold Up Pants"	169
27	There Are Only Two Masters in the Entire World Who Can Help Me	182
28	What? No Dinner Tonight?	195
	Epilogue	199

ACKNOWLEDGMENTS

There are so many people that I need to thank for helping me with this book. The list is absolutely endless. Okay, maybe just very long. There are hundreds of them. Friends, great friends, family, authors, editors, spiritual teachers, spiritual students, publishing teachers, writing teachers, marketing teachers, random people who helped me sometimes without even knowing and people who were sent by the universe as teachers and guides. On days when you think that the world is bad, I invite you to think of all the people that ever helped you, many times without expecting anything in return.
I would just mention a few of them without whom this book would never be written.
I would like to thank Beth who if it wasn't for her question I would not write the English version. Jacquie, Mike and Tehila who were the first to edit my English version. Josh and Johanna who lead the writing groups I joined. Sylvia who was giving great suggestions to improve the story. My dear friends who supported me in the process, Karen, Sam, Diane, Alex, Ed, Meredith, Brenda, Diana and Fabienne. Special thanks to my editors Jessica Marrero & Glenda Shenkal and my cover designed Sagi Meir.

The gangster Al Capone has been quoted saying:

"You can go a long way with a smile.

You can go a lot farther with a smile and a gun."

Is this really the only way to get a lot farther?

INTRODUCTION
CAN A WARRIOR FIND PEACE?

Are you a warrior? I suspect you will answer: No. According to Wikipedia, a warrior is a person skilled in combat or warfare, especially within the context of a tribal or clan-based society that recognizes a separate warrior class. You don't fall under this definition, but I'm not talking about this kind of warrior.

My definition of a warrior is someone who is steered by fear. Someone who is worried about the future, finds it hard to fully enjoy the present, and many times either wishes he could relive the past or is angry for making too many mistakes; "If only I said... If only I didn't... If I could go back in time and..."

If you feel that something is wrong with your life, then you are a warrior. Some warriors feel that they aren't attractive enough. Some warriors think they aren't talented enough. Most warriors are not happy with their job, and wish they had more money. Warriors don't believe they deserve what it is they most want, at least not without a fight.

You may also feel that something is wrong with the people around you. "If only people could see me the way I really am and value and appreciate me."

If you're a warrior, you can't trust people and secretly, desperately feel you could use Aladdin's genie to give you three wishes to change your life.

So, are you a warrior?

If you're still not sure, please visit the quiz on my website: http://oneleggedseagull.com/test-yourself-are-you-a-warrior.

If you are a warrior, I have some surprises for you that can help you create the reality you want.

How did I come to write about warriors? In order to answer this question, I need to share with you a personal story from my past. Sometimes, you need to face an extreme situation in order to see who and what you are. My story starts on the day that I had the sight of my gun locked on another person, and I was ready to shoot him. It happened almost twenty years ago, when I was a soldier.

Being a solider is not an easy task; the problem is, you don't get to choose your enemies. In the better scenario, you feel that you are fighting to protect your home, family, friends and country. In the worse scenario, you are fighting only because some politician told you that the people on other side of the war are your enemy.

In the better scenario, you chose to join the army. Maybe you were looking for an adventure, maybe you liked the risk. In the worse scenario, you are there because your country has mandatory army service, and now you're old enough to go off and fight for your nation. Some countries require it of all young people over a certain age.

However you came to be a soldier, when you face an enemy, any enemy, you experience the feeling of: "It's either me or them." For a soldier this is a matter of life or death. One moment of weakness and he is the one who's going to get taken down by the next bullet; or even worse, maybe a terrorist will sneak into a civilian neighborhood and plant a bomb that kills innocents--on *his* watch.

You might ask yourself: "Why is he telling me about that? I'm not a soldier, and I never pointed a gun at anyone." Yet, you probably have similar experiences often in your own life, even though you never went to an official war. You feel that same terrible pressure whenever you fight with another person. It doesn't need to be a matter of life and death. It can be as small as who gets to decide what to do next, whose fault something was, or any other drama you go through.

In a nut shell, the feeling of "It's either me or them" is the fuel that drives any warrior in his wars, whether he is a soldier or not. It's in our cellular memory, a reminder of times when we had to fight in order to survive another day. If you look closely, most everyday dramas feel to you like they're a life or death matter, even if they're not. In the moment of a fight, you forget that your "temporary enemy" is, most of the time, actually your friend. Think about your last fight with someone close to you. What did you fight about? Was it really that important? Was it a life or death matter? Why was it so important for you to win? Why couldn't you let the other side have a moment of triumph? Why couldn't you both win?

If you often have internal or external conflicts in your life, then you are a warrior. And warriors can't find their inner peace.

I didn't used to think that I was a warrior. Yes, I had some disagreements with others from time to time. Yes, I saw how other people can be wrong or unfair. Yes, I was mostly restless; aren't we all? And come to think of it, when people used to ask me: "what do you want?" I used to say: "Just some peace of mind, just make this brain stop thinking." But was I a warrior? Me? No way! Or at least, that's what I thought.

Then during my mandatory army service something happened. One day, in a hostile village, four friends from my platoon were ambushed by a gang of teenagers who pelted them with a bombardment of stones. The situation was so dire that we barely managed to rescue my friends before they were lynched by that gang. When I saw the terrified looks in my friend's eyes, I thought: "Damn, we could have lost them if we were just a few minutes later showing up. Damn, it could have been me that was under attack."

The next day it was my turn to patrol in the same street. We walked up the hill between the old brick houses on the narrow path. I was very nervous and alert and made sure that my team was ready for any surprise. One hour into the patrol, a little kid appeared in front of me and threw a small stone. This was exactly how the incident had started the previous day. I could see again in my imagination the eyes of my horrified friends when we rescued them. The hair on my hand bristled and I squeezed the barrel of my gun. When the next teenager showed up with a bigger stone, I locked my scope on him--he was the human target--and I was ready to shoot. I was a kid too, not even twenty, and he was the enemy.

When I share this story with people, they often say: "You did the right thing. You had the right to shoot the boy; that kid was going to attack you, and you had to defend yourself." While this perspective might be accurate from the warrior's point of view, the need to be right is what many times stands between you and your inner peace. So in that split second, with my trembling finger on the trigger, ready to shoot the kid, I stopped and looked inside. I could feel my anger; anger for being attacked; anger for what those villagers had done to my friends the day before; anger for the necessity of having to be there at all, a vulnerable soldier in a hostile village. I could also feel my fear. Maybe it wasn't an immediately life threatening situation, but it could easily escalate to that level, and I wasn't letting that happen, like my friends did on their patrol.

Then fortunately, the boy dropped his stone and ran away. Most people would say that he saw my gun and got scared. This is probably true. But I see it from another perspective. From where I stand now, he ran away because his purpose in helping me see inside myself was finished.

The way I understand things, the real use of an enemy (or a loved one, when you fight with a friend or family member) is to be a teacher. That boy mirrored for me my inner shadows, my reactions and my own fear. And once I could see what he was showing me, he could leave my life--in peace.

I found out that day that an enemy can be a trigger, to either a war or a growth process that will lead to inner peace.

For many years I observed myself and others in similar situations. Not only in the army, but also in relationships, at work and on the road. It was easy to watch and learn, since there is always drama around somewhere. I used my observations to create a path that will bring me the serenity I yearned for. In the process, I realized that while life surprises us with different events, we always have two paths we can choose.

The first way of walking is the warrior path. This is a fear-based path, characterized by being ready to fight and protect yourself at any time. This is the path I walked as a soldier, and the path many singles and couples I've met were walking without knowing there is another way.

The second road is the path of the creative artist, the path of love for yourself and compassion for others; the road by which you can shape your own reality. I discuss this path in detail in this book.

It wasn't easy to learn how to abandon my warrior habits, and it took me more than a decade to find my own way on the artist path. But once I found how to do it, I knew that I had to share what I had learned with you. I see so much drama around, so much emotional pain, and I can't just ignore it. I want to support the ones who've had enough of their pain and are ready for a change.

That's how I came to write this fable. In this story, I'm going to take you on an internal journey similar to the one that I walked, so you can find your own natural direction into joy. In this book I have drawn for you the complete map that will show you how to avoid conflicts, how to create win-win games, how to transform an enemy into a friend, and how to get back on the artist path when you feel yourself sliding once again into warrior consciousness. You'll learn how to use your weaknesses as advantages, how to see that even nothing can be something, and what the one approach is, that can disarm almost any attacker. Once you experience all of that through the story and the characters, you will be able to uplift yourself so you can live your life to your full potential.

You see, while the warrior believes that in order to achieve his goals he needs to fight and work hard, the artist avoids the struggle, but still he doesn't wait for magic to happen to him… he creates it.

My story starts like my life and probably yours, with some drama and conflicts. The characters feel and act like warriors. Drama can be good, if it's a trigger for a change. Being patient with the drama is one of the keys to dissolve it. When the characters realize they need a change, they look for someone to show them the way.

When you read this story, you will be able to find your own path through your personal dramas and walk together with JJ, Sara, David, Gill, Ehud, May and Simon on a self empowerment journey. Let this story be your own personal coaching system, which you use to uplift your life.

May you find your own path to be at peace,

Joey Avniel.

1 - MY WEAKNESS MIGHT SOMEDAY BECOME AN ADVANTAGE

It was Friday afternoon and JJ was ready for a war. Not the kind of war where you shoot someone, but the kind where you wish you could. He sat in his pajamas in the middle of his living room, scratching his crooked nose, a reminder from a long forgotten fist fight. *If only I could go back to sleep and forget about everything*, he thought while releasing a sigh. His always-stubbly-chin slumped toward his chest and his wide forehead rested on an open palm. His brown eyes were closed.

On Monday, two of his best gaming developers had quit without notice. On Tuesday, rumors about the delay in his project, the next generation gaming console, crashed the company's stock on NASDAQ. On Wednesday, the board of directors asked him to explain the situation, making JJ feel like a student called to the principal's office. On Thursday, the CEO announced that their biggest competitor, Sony, might beat them to the marketplace by releasing a new console first. This was the worst week in JJ's career.

While changing from his PJ's into jeans, he looked around the room. How could he release his rage? Maybe punching something would make him feel better. He glanced at the running horses in the framed puzzle hanging on the wall. Nah, he'd spent too many hours putting it together. Maybe he should attack the mountains of flowcharts, project plans, and balance sheets on his desk? A little smile crossed his face. They reminded him of the skyline in midtown Manhattan. Leaving New York and moving back to Israel a few years ago was a difficult step for him. But he couldn't stay far away from the only family he had, his older sister, Sara, after their parents had passed away.

The only other things in the room that he could break would be the sagging sofa, his computer chair, or the TV couch. The flat screen TV, his laptop and the Italian glass table were out of the question. Even though it had been his ex-girlfriend's bad idea to buy that ugly table, it had still cost more than a month's salary. On the table he had a half-empty cup of coffee that he'd planned to finish, the company cell phone, and the land line speaker phone that was playing an annoying on-hold song. The only potential victim there was the porcelain vase with the fake flowers, but that had been his mom's last present.

He sat down again and chewed his thumb. Since childhood, he'd been skilled at finding the easiest way to solve a problem. That's why the company had put him in charge of their most complicated project. If he had a dime for every time he heard someone say to him, "I can't believe I didn't think of that," he'd be rich. Most of his friends and coworkers called him The Wiz. He liked being considered a Wiz. At thirty one, being the youngest and most highly compensated product manager at his company was always a source of pride. "We're the future of gaming," he told all his friends. Unfortunately, on that Friday, he was far from feeling like a Wiz. The gap between his normal state of mind and his present state of mind was growing by the minute. It approached the distance between his previous home on Central Park West and his current, modest house, near Tel Aviv. Once again he learned that in the absence of light at the end of the tunnel, darkness is all you see. Wizards are expected to create magic. Would he be able to?

ONE-LEGGED SEAGULL

* * * * *

Just a week before, everything had been business as usual. On Saturday afternoon, JJ had gone to Tel Aviv's silver-sanded beach. The cloudy skies promised a festival of red and orange hues when the sun set toward its watery bed. He sat down on the warm sand and prepared for meditation. He set his thin body straight; the same body he described on dating sites like *JDATE* as athletic. His search for inner peace, which had started soon after he had finished his mandatory army service, by now included endless books, retreats, and workshops. It had been mostly successful; however, a decent meditation remained out of reach. After trying for thirty minutes he accepted that, as usual, his stormy memories were louder than the waves' calming sound.

He rose and shook sand off his shorts and "I Love NY" t-shirt. The faint sound of drums coming from a nearby beach made him start free-style dancing. When he got tired he found a rock to sit on, and pulled his laptop from his bag to check emails. He was still laughing at a dirty joke that Sara had emailed as he replaced the laptop in its bag. As he pulled out a camera, his cell rang. He checked the screen hoping it wasn't a work call and was relieved to see his nephew's smile. It was as pure as the first baby smile that Gill had flashed him almost fourteen years ago; a toothless smile, but full of pure optimism. Gill had bestowed the name "JJ" upon him due to a toddler's pronunciation difficulties. Since that time, the name, "JJ," had stuck.

"Hey, Uncle JJ. Watsup?"

"You know, I'm at the beach."

Gill chuckled. "Oh, yeah. I totally forgot it's your date with the seagulls."

JJ set up the tripod. "Yup. Is everything alright? Do you need anything?"

"No, don't worry. I need your advice again about that girl I told you about, Michelle. But it's cool. It can wait 'till our Friday basketball game. I don't want to ruin your quality time with the birds."

JJ already had his camera pointed at the sky. "Are you sure?"

"Yeah, it's not an emergency. Have fun. Talk to you soon."

"Yeah, you too, take care." JJ hung up. He took some quick shots of the gliding seagulls. For a second he got excited when he thought he saw the one-legged seagull, but he was wrong. He gazed at the sky and thought about the bird that had changed his perspective about having weaknesses.

On one of his regular beach excursions, he had brought along some bread, hoping the birds would eat from his hand. Only one of them was bold enough. Every few minutes the very same seagull would dive down, snatch a piece of bread, and quickly return to the safety of the skies. It circled for a minute, then returned for more bread. The other seagulls seemed to just watch from a safe distance.

When JJ went home that night, he downloaded the photographs onto his computer. He couldn't stop thinking about the daring seagull. *What had made that particular seagull braver than the others?* He zoomed in on an image of that seagull. It was then he noticed that it had only one leg. The poor bird had probably had a horrible accident. Because of this disability, it couldn't remain in the safety of the seagulls' comfort zone, away from people. It had to adapt, find other ways to survive.

This made JJ think about his own Achilles' heel. Dyslexia had made reading and writing a challenge for him. Schoolwork was more difficult than for his classmates and sometimes even felt impossible. Back when he was younger there was less awareness of his condition. Much like the seagull that had to take the road less traveled, JJ had learned to look for ways to conquer his weakness. By doing so, he developed new talents. Being able to put together a whole picture in his head, from just few clues, was one of them.

JJ's best friend at elementary school had once asked, "How come school is so easy for you? I wish I could be an A student like you. If only I was smarter…"

JJ smiled. "I'm not smarter than you, pal, and school is anything but easy for me. I have to find my own ways to learn since I can't write as fast as the teachers speak, and my memory is always overwhelmed. It's sometimes frustrating, and sometimes like a game. I need to be very creative in order to find ways to concentrate. You can't understand, because you're normal. Mom says that my weakness might someday become an advantage."

* * * * *

Another missed call from work on JJ's cell made him shake his head unhappily and return to the distressing present. The bright sunlight that peeked invitingly through the front window, made every cell of his reddish skin scream that he should be spending this sunny day outdoors, rather than working on Friday, a weekend day in Israel. In order to quiet the accusations shouting in his head, he turned on the TV and switched to the *National Geographic* channel. If he couldn't be enjoying real nature, at least he could have it in the background. His cell phone rang for what seemed like the millionth time that day. He looked at the screen. Not surprisingly, it was the director of his project.

"Shit," he said out loud, and silenced the ring. "Hello, is anybody there?" he said into the land line's speakerphone. But, it continued playing the on-hold song. His right hand reached toward the table but froze half way through the gesture; he wouldn't find a cigarette pack there. He had quit smoking months ago. "Damn!" he mumbled. The cell phone rang again, this time it was the CEO.

2 - THREE PAIRS OF FRANTICALLY WAVING ARMS

A few miles from JJ's house, a dark blue Grand Cherokee SUV was speeding down the highway, changing lanes between cars stuck in traffic.

"I hate slow drivers who insist on staying in the left lane," David mumbled, while giving the finger to another driver. "Son of a---"

After a glimpse in the rearview mirror, where he saw Gill, his teenage son, sitting in the back seat, he didn't finish. He smoothed his brown hair with his big palm and glanced at Sara, his wife. She didn't turn her head to look at him. "How, exactly, is it my fault again?" he asked, and blinked his almond-shaped eyes in frustration.

Sara pulled her short dress down over her knees. "I didn't say it's your fault, David, but we also can't let Gill fail. I need you to work with me here, but I feel that your job is the only thing you care about."

He changed lanes again. "Do you really have to keep nagging me about my job? If I could, I'd have quit yesterday and found a more relaxing one."

Sara used the small mirror behind the sun visor to powder her pale cheeks and fix her red hair. It was already perfect, but she had to keep herself busy. *Think positive*, she repeated to herself; *look at the glass as half full*. But negativity took over. "I thought you liked your job, Mr. big shot. You always brag about your wins."

He turned his sad eyes to Sara, and nearly crashed into the car ahead of him. "Do you think that I like defending careless drivers that should be behind bars? That's not why I went to law school. I wanted to change the world, but somehow the world changed me." He pulled his sunglasses from the top of his head and put them over his eyes before continuing. "Someone has to pay off the loans you insisted we take. It's not my fault I have to work overtime just to make ends meet. I'd love to play a bigger role in Gill's life, but when I come home exhausted all I want is some peace of mind. Give me that and you'll make me the happiest person on earth."

Sara took a deep breath and put her hands on her thighs. Tears filled her eyes. "I don't want to fight with you, but don't put it all on me." She looked at him, but he had already become mute, as usual. "What happened to the charming David I married twenty years ago? Why are you so bitter? I know you have to work hard and my teacher's salary is peanuts, but you still have a family. When was the last time you said something nice to me? Or the last time you bought me some flowers? Or any gift for that matter?" She bit her quivering lip and put a hand over her mouth. "Sorry, I shouldn't say that. I can't control myself. I'm so worried about Gill that I can't think straight. You know I love you. I just feel frustrated having to deal with Gill on my own. I need your support as well."

She put her hand on David's knee, but he kept his gaze on the road. She removed her hand and looked back at Gill, who wore a headset plugged into his player. He was using two pens to drum along to the music. "Gill, you know I love you and want only what's best for you. Why do you have to make me feel like I'm nothing but a nag? I'm just trying to help you, baby."

Gill pointed at the headphones in his ears. "Can't hear you Mom," he shouted, and closed his honey-brown eyes. She always said he'd become deaf because his music was so loud, but he'd rather have that than listen to her lectures on studying more or behaving better. He just wanted to be himself, not a better version of himself or of anyone else.

He looked out the window at the shrinking skyline of Tel Aviv. He wanted his problems to disappear like the big towers by the far beach. He wished he could stop thinking about Michelle. She was the prettiest girl at school, and again, someone had asked her out before he had the courage to. He wished he could forget about his parents, a father who rarely talked and a mother who never stopped. If there was such a thing as a parenting school, they'd both fail. Not only that, if a bolt of lightning were to destroy his school, he wouldn't be sorry. In fact, it'd be an added bonus if all the teachers were inside having one of their stupid meetings when it happened.

Gill glanced at his parents and sighed. Maybe Uncle JJ can help us. He always has great ideas.

* * * * *

JJ finally heard the voice of the Easy Chips' customer support representative coming through the speaker phone. "Yes, Mr. Cohen, sorry to keep you waiting. Are you still there?"

He checked the time; he had been on hold for more than ten minutes. "Don't worry, I'm not going anywhere, not until I get answers."

"Excellent, Mr. Cohen," she said, with a sickly sweet voice. "I checked with the shipping department. The shift manager assured me they're processing your shipment even as we speak."

"I've been given this very same assurance many times in the past week," he said. "Can you just be straight with me?"

"Mr. Cohen, believe me, I'm telling you everything I know. You'll get the order next week."

He almost crushed his phone with his shaky fist. "I already bought your false promises, I'm through with that. I needed those damn chips yesterday or I'll lose my job, so don't bullshit me! Can't you understand how desperate my situation has become?"

"Mr. Cohen, there's no need to raise your voice. We're doing everything possible to deliver your chips."

His eyes wandered over to the *National Geographic* Channel. *It's a shame*, he thought, *that the lion on the screen didn't chase this Easy Chips representative instead of the poor zebra.* "You don't understand. My whole project is shut down; twenty-three people are standing around waiting for chips that should've arrived a week ago. If Sony releases their console first, I won't even need your stupid chips, since I'll be on the street. Can you help me resolve this or not?"

"Look, Mr. Cohen, I'm just the messenger," she said, her voice as calm as if she had been selecting a tablecloth for that evening's dinner. "You know what they say, don't shoot---"

"Oh, come on! Really? Now you're gonna start throwing clichés at me?" JJ's voice trembled as he interrupted her. Whoever said you shouldn't shoot the messenger obviously hadn't encountered this woman.

"Is there anything else I can do for you today, Mr. Cohen?" she asked, in a bored voice.

"Yes, just stop Mr. Cohening me! You're completely useless." He concluded the conversation by hanging up on her. If he couldn't win, at least he could protest.

JJ could feel a vein popping out of his temple. "You sound just like Dad," he could hear Sara's voice in his head. Many years ago, when she had to bail him out after another fight in a bar, he promised her that he'd change. And he had changed. All of his consistent self-help work had started paying off. Conflicts like this were rare; most people who knew him would be shocked to see him losing it like this. With an exhaled breath, he tried to release some of the steam that had been building up. He reached out for the cup on the table. "Damn..." the coffee was already cold. His cell phone rang again.

* * * * *

A lion's roar followed by a scream sucked his attention back to the TV. It took a few seconds to realize that the source of the scream was outside his house, not from the TV. It was the screech of tires squealing to a sharp stop. This was an extraordinary sound for his quiet, suburban Tel Aviv neighborhood. When he lived in New York, a siren couldn't make him leave his La-Z-Boy. In Israel, things were different. An intense feeling clouded the air, as if another war was just around the corner. In an environment like this, everything looked and sounded more extreme. He jumped up and rushed to the front window to see what had caused the commotion.

He pushed aside the curtains, surprising a pigeon which escaped in panic from the old oak tree in his front yard. The neighbor across the street was washing his car, his kids climbing in their tree house. An elderly couple walked holding hands, and two teenagers jogged in the shaded street; none of this explained the fuss. Another scan of the street exposed a dark blue SUV parked at the end of two skid marks. JJ peered at the car through his window. His gaze followed three pairs of frantically waving arms. The arms seemed to be dancing but he knew, even though he couldn't hear the voices, that harsh words were being exchanged.

At once, he forgot about his project and his attention shifted to the SUV. His body tightened as the passengers descended from the car, slamming their doors in perfect harmony. He followed the small group as they left the vehicle heading toward his front door.

"Gimme a break, Mom! Not gonna happen!" Gill yelled kicking a garbage can. "I don't owe you anything."

JJ felt the hair on his hand bristle in reaction to his beloved nephew's attitude. When he was Gill's age, no properly-raised child would ever show his parents this kind of disrespect.

David, JJ's brother-in-law, spoke in an aggravated voice, his index finger trembling as he pointed at his son. "Hey, young man, watch your attitude! You aren't talking to one of your friends. We deserve a little bit of respect."

"Who wants to be a friend of yours anyway?" Gill asked, and raised his round chin in a rebellious, defiant manner.

Sara's eyes looked like clouds before a tropical storm and her gaze said what her mouth could not. Usually, her short legs moved quickly, trying to keep up with David's long strides, but today she seemed to drag herself along in a discouraged way.

JJ knew that they could easily continue this fight for another hour, but the doorstep made them call a temporary cease-fire. The door buzzer sounded, announcing the end of another round. On his way to the front door, he made a quick stop in the living room. In order to prevent the room from looking like a messy office, he hurriedly shoved papers into every available drawer. He wasn't sure whether the light pressure in his chest was due to frustration from work, his family's fight, or the sudden onset of a heart attack.

3 - MY GREEN BELT STORY

JJ yanked the door open and his family marched in as solemnly as if they were arriving at a funeral. David entered first and went straight into the living room. "You don't want to know," he blurted out with a sigh. Five seconds later, he crashed on the sofa and disappeared behind a newspaper. His legs, sliding nervously back and forth across the glass table, were the only part of him still visible.

Sara entered the room shortly after her husband. She avoided her brother's eyes. Her usual warm hug was replaced by a distant one that lasted about a second; she abruptly snuck off into the kitchen to start preparing their traditional Friday dinner.

"Hey, Uncle JJ," Gill said softly, as he passed through the doorway. He too avoided looking into JJ's eyes, his gaze dropping to the floor. His usual enthusiasm had failed to show up today. JJ noticed Gill's sloppy attire: his button-down shirt, which usually dared not escape his pants, was tucked too deep on the left side, and completely untucked on the right.

I can deal with the adults later, JJ thought, as he gently squeezed Gill's shoulder and escorted him out to the backyard basketball court. JJ had converted his private parking spot into a court of sorts by fastening a large metal ring to the side of his house for the hoop. That was his special place to bond with Gill. Each time they dribbled, it felt like the cypresses lining the house jumped with every bounce of the ball.

Gill started to shoot some balls while JJ stretched. He watched Gill jump, almost dunking the ball. The times when JJ let Gill win were long gone. Nowadays Gill, who wasn't yet fourteen, was only half an inch shorter than JJ's five foot nine, and would most likely grow taller.

During last week's game Gill had said, "Admit it, Uncle, you're a big *Center* caged in the body of a *Smurf*." Then he smiled mischievously at JJ. "Uncle, listen!" He froze, tilting his head and cupping his hand against his ear. "Can you hear this? It's me growing. Out-rebound me while you still can," he whispered, as he fast-breaked past JJ, quick as a cheetah.

JJ took a deep breath and filled his lungs with the expected authoritativeness of a mature uncle. While exhaling, he scanned Gill top-to-bottom with the thoroughness of an X-ray machine. He tried to identify the source of Gill's problem but it appeared that apart from the sour face and the wayward shirt, there were no clues. *What trouble did you get yourself into this time?* The thought traveled to the tip of JJ's tongue, but he was careful not to verbalize it. The last thing he wanted was to force his nephew on the defensive. JJ put his hand on his own chest, tightened his eyes and jaw, pretending to feel hurt. "What's the matter, kid? Not happy to see your uncle today?"

"It's not you, Uncle JJ," Gill answered in a barely audible voice. "Life sucks and my stupid parents are just making it worse."

"Is that what you think? Listen buddy, put on your basketball uniform pronto, and if I don't see some toothy grins soon, I'll have to massively kick your butt."

Gill's eyes answered, *Not gonna happen, not today.* He reluctantly flashed a weak smile and they both went inside to change their clothes. Gill put on his blue "I love Uncle JJ" t-shirt that had been washed during the week so that it would be ready for its Friday performance. JJ slipped into a pair of shorts and sported his own t-shirt, which proudly boasted the title, "World's Best Uncle." This special t-shirt was a custom-made birthday gift from Gill. Gill and JJ knew their shirts were silly, yet they had become a must-wear for their ritual backyard one-on-one basketball games.

A few minutes later, uncle and nephew were engaged in a fierce basketball duel. After a successful shot by JJ, Gill began to pour his heart out. "I wish I was dead," he said, and passed the ball to his uncle.

JJ dried the sweat from his forehead. *When did Gill leave the happy "Kids' Club" to join the morose "Teenagers' Club"?* Back in his day, it took at least sixteen years before one was granted membership into this bitter society. JJ paused, searching for the right words. "Can you please start the story from the beginning?"

"Mom should've been a woodpecker. I mean, the way she's constantly picking at me. My semester grades have only two, maybe three, *F*'s. The problem is that the rest of my grades aren't much better. The counselor met with Mom and said that I have a lot of potential, but if I don't improve my grades I might have to be put in a special class or maybe repeat this year. Since then, Mom is picking and picking at me. I'm grounded, my plasma and computer are gone, and my allowance is cut. Why doesn't anyone mention the *A*'s I got in gymnastics and art?" Gill's eyes flickered in a mixture of frustration and anger as the dam he had built up collapsed, and a stream of words washed through the backyard.

JJ opened his mouth in an effort to express some compassionate words, but changed his mind when he saw that Gill wasn't done yet.

"If they take me out of my class, I'll lose all the friends I've known since kindergarten. I'll become the laughing stock of the entire neighborhood. Why can't they understand that I'm good at some things, but just not good with exams?"

Gill's look reminded JJ of a lost puppy stuck in the middle of a highway. Gill threw the ball, but his famous, deadly fade-away shot didn't even hit the backboard.

"I know exactly what you mean," JJ said, while catching the airball and trying to pass Gill on his way to the rim. "I also had a problem with exams when I was your age."

Gill raised his eyebrows. "Are you kidding? Mom always talks about how Uncle JJ never prepared for any exam, and come the big day, got all A's." Gill used his praise as a distraction to steal the ball from his uncle's hands.

"First of all, your mother is world famous for being a serial exaggerator," JJ said, trying to hide his annoyance with Gill's sneaky trick, "and secondly, life is full of exams and tests, not only in school." He stretched out his arms just enough to block Gill's shot. He stole the ball, took a shot and missed. That was fine, but he couldn't afford to miss helping Gill. He took a bottle of water from the top of a small bench and threw it toward Gill. "You need to drink, kiddo."

While opening the bottle Gill said, "Yeah, tell me about it. I keep failing the 'girl' exam. I told you about Michelle. I'm crazy about her. She doesn't want me though, and the girls I don't like won't leave me alone."

The sun was dropping slowly behind the treetops. Millions of thoughts overwhelmed JJ, racing in his head like bumper cars in an amusement park. He had to find the right strategy to encourage Gill. A few minutes and a couple of misses later, JJ finally made a swish shot. He also felt an idea swishing around in his head, but before he could share it, he'd have to check on the rest of the family. "Okay, I'm officially out of oxygen. We can call it a week," he said, and sent Gill to take a shower while he joined Sara in the kitchen.

"How are you doing, sis? Everything cool?" JJ asked. The spicy smell wafting out of the roast beef pot followed by Sara's sneeze answered his question. The more upset she was, the more pepper she put in her dishes.

With her back to him, she said, "Cut the crap, JJ! Did Gill tell you that they want him to repeat this year?" It seemed that today Sara wasn't feeling her usual fondness for small talk. "It's a continuous battle, he won't do his homework, won't prepare for exams, and won't help me with house chores. Everything I ask him to do ends in a fight." She paused, looking in the direction of the kitchen door, and into the living room where David was still engrossed in his newspaper. She raised her voice. "He's exactly like his father. I have two warriors fighting a war of attrition, a war I have no chance of winning." She swallowed in frustration as her wet eyes made first contact with her brother. "JJ, my life's an endless struggle. I have no energy left!"

JJ touched her shoulder softly and kissed her forehead. She inhaled deeply, escaped from JJ's oncoming hug, and headed straight for the fridge to pull out some tomatoes. As he sat on a counter bar stool, JJ's heart, overheated from exertion, beat wildly. He had known that this visit would turn into a family therapy session as soon as he first spotted them through the window. It had happened before. When Sara was under pressure, she tended to fall apart. Gill's failure was just the tip of the iceberg.

While peeling an orange, he thought about the days when he, too, used to be a warrior. Then a story helped him to change the course of his life. While dealing with the *Easy Chips* representative earlier that day he had fallen back into his warrior ways. Lately he had felt like his hat was running out of rabbits, and now he had the crisis in his project. The next few weeks were crucial if he didn't want to lose his job. But the damn chips were delayed and there was no workable alternative to the situation he found himself in.

His director's words came back to him. "If I didn't know you, I'd think you're an amateur and not my omnipotent Wiz." Yes, he needed to remind himself of that story's message. It would get him back on the artist path. And now was an excellent opportunity to introduce it to his family.

Gill appeared in the kitchen after taking his shower. "Uncle JJ, can I please have a cinnamon cookie?"

"Sure," JJ said, chewing a slice of the orange and ignoring the bitter look his sister shot at him.

Gill winked at JJ. "Mom, it's okay, I can eat the whole kitchen after the game I just had with Uncle JJ."

JJ left them to take a short shower - a habit developed while serving in the army. Four minutes later, refreshed and redressed, he escorted Gill and Sara to the living room. "Have I ever told you my Green Belt story?" he asked with the most enthusiastic tone he could find, left over from happier days.

"A story?" Gill asked. "I'm not in the mood for a story."

David turned the page of his newspaper as if saying, "I'm not interested." But JJ wasn't fooled by David. JJ knew that deep down inside David would be content with hearing a story because then he wouldn't have to talk. Sara, who had heard her younger brother tell his first story using baby babble, bit her upper lip. Her eyes said, "Nice try JJ, but it's not gonna work today."

JJ gave an inquiring look. "Why?"

"I haven't heard this story, but right now a story isn't exactly what we need. I know what you're trying to do, but we have so much stuff going on. We need solutions, not stories."

"Solutions for what, sis?"

"You really want to know? Okay. Gill's not studying. David didn't get the promotion he's owed and has to deal with the arrogant bastard, Danny Cordova, who stole it. And I'm the favorite punching bag of both Gill and David here."

JJ thought that if she were a dragon she'd blow fire through her nostrils. Hoping to diffuse her feelings, he hugged her curvy waist. "Look, sis, just give my story a chance. You might see things differently. Maybe you'll find that things aren't as bad as they seem. Maybe you'll even find a solution. In the worst case scenario, you'll gain a short break from the fights you hate so much and you'll be able to enjoy a good story. In any case you have no choice because you're going to hear this story whether you like it or not. You'd better get comfortable and relax, since in the next hour or so you're my captive audience."

David seemed to realize that JJ meant business. He sighed, put down his newspaper and made room on the couch for Sara. She sniffed, then collapsed heavily beside her husband. Gill grabbed a chair, spun it around, and sat with his chest leaning into the backrest. He was the number one fan of JJ's tales.

Gill grinned as JJ opened by saying what he always said when he told a story. "Every word in this story is true, except for what I changed, forgot, left out, added or exaggerated." JJ took a quick sip of water and continued. "Many years ago, in a far, far-away kingdom, there was a brave, young Kung Fu warrior named Ehud."

Gill's face wore an annoyed expression. "Come on, Uncle! Be serious for a change."

"Why? What have I done?"

"I know you too well. Your stories always happen to you, not to someone else. If this were the real story, then you'd be Ehud. So, put your character on and stop wasting our time, before I get bored, dig it?"

"Okay, I'm sorry, you caught me," JJ said, unapologetically. He knew he could count on Gill to notice the fake opening.

"Yes, brother, why don't you start with the real story already?" A gleam of a smile raced across Sara's face.

David stared at his brother-in-law and nodded, as if saying, "Well, go ahead, I'm waiting."

JJ was satisfied. Just a minute ago he'd had to force them to listen. They had been so absorbed in their own drama, that they resisted any attempt to shift their attention. Fortunately his little trick had worked, and now they were the ones pushing for him to start.

He closed his eyes and listened to the heartbeat of each one of his listeners. Is it possible that God creates crisis in our lives just for moments like this? If so, there is no doubt He knows His job. JJ took a deep breath and cleared his mind. He felt as if his body shed its weight and pressure. He dropped his familiar sense of space and time, until he reached the point where he was no longer in the room with his family. Then he inhaled deeply until he felt his body shifting into a new shape like a balloon. His mind filled with his new character's thoughts; a new setting sprouted up around him.

When he opened his eyes, he was no longer JJ; he was Ehud, a young Kung Fu warrior.

4 - IT TAKES TWO LEGS TO KICK

It takes two legs to kick. Every kid knows that. While one leg does the standing, the other one does the kicking. I keep thinking of a scene from the movie, "The Karate Kid." In this particular scene, the hero, who injured his left leg in the semifinals, is now at the last stage of the championship. He steadies himself on his right leg in the famous crane stance position. With his arms outstretched, eyes focused on his opponent, he leaps impressively into the air, kicks and lands with his right foot. My opinion of this maneuver: im-pos-sible! It's nothing but a movie stunt. No matter how many times I tried the crane kick, I never succeeded. I did succeed once… in landing on my nose in the playground at school and getting a free pass to the nurse's office. Normal people like me, who aren't directly related to cranes, need to use both legs to launch a proper kick.

Usually, a righty fighter will choose to kick with the right leg. However, this exposes a vulnerability to the opponent who can now take advantage of the fact that the kicker is standing unbalanced on the weaker leg. So if you are going to kick someone, I recommend that you make sure that your kick meets its target. It's safer that way.

I'm different, a righty, born into a family of lefties. They are all lefties! I am almost certain that even our dog, May, is a lefty. Maybe that is why almost five years ago, at the age of eight, I started to favor my left foot when kicking the ball in soccer. My right leg remains my strong leg and provides me with a solid base, but five years and a million games have turned my left leg into the more accurate kicker of the two. And so, I feel more comfortable kicking with my left leg; this means I stand on my strong leg while kicking. That gives me an edge over my opponent, which...

"Ehud, stop daydreaming! We're up. It's our turn for the test." The kid next to me yanked me out of my daydream with an elbow jab to the ribs.

It was a steamy afternoon, one of those end-of-spring-beginning-of-summer days. My dojo was holding belt qualification tests and I was up for the Green Belt test. The temperature inside the dojo was even more intense than it was outside. The body heat emanating from all of the people coupled with the still air, made the auditorium feel like a pizza oven. The loyal old AC system, which wasn't used to cooling so many bodies, gave its all. It emitted a loud groan every now and then, followed by a noisy sound like it was kicking a wall. It was as if the AC was trying to scare the heat away. Unfortunately, it was a losing battle, and the coaches, students, friends, and parents who had come to watch paid the price in gallons of sweat.

I threw a last, hopeful look at the picture of the dojo's founder hanging on the white wall between two windows. I tried to draw strength from the image of this Chinese master. He was standing tall in a black suit, and although he looked gentle, one could see the power in his eyes. His stare alone could probably freeze his opponent's blood. I kissed my Yin-Yang pendant for luck, and jumped onto the blue and red mats. My pulse was racing, and my heart felt like it might explode and pop out of my chest at any moment.

About fifteen seconds and a million heartbeats later, the coach signaled for the test to begin. For the next few minutes we students became one body. We were a twelve-kid fighting machine, practicing kata after kata, kicking, jumping, defending and attacking invisible rivals. A kata is a sequence of fighting moves, kind of a Kung Fu dance. I don't like katas any more than I like dancing, which isn't a lot.

A few years ago, mom had encouraged me to sign up for a dance class. I went in one day to give it a try and show off my dance potential. The instructor wasn't at all impressed with my skills. After watching me for a few minutes, he flatly stated, "You're a dance dyslexic. You can't spell out the correct moves in the proper sequence, and you really can't convert them into dance sentences. I think you should consider a different activity, something other than dance." Even though I was too embarrassed to ask for the exact translation of what he said, I got his message: *I stink at dancing*.

When I forgot the next move of the kata, I glanced around so that I might catch up with the rest of the group. To my surprise, even though my timing was slightly off on a few instances, my performance ranged from not-too-bad, to almost artful. I'd need just a pinch of luck and I could pass this.

Following the katas, we each had two kumite rounds. The definition of kumite is "free form fighting, with enough rules to make injuries unlikely." The first round was against a student of a similar skill level and the second one was against a Green Belt student. For me, kumite was too much like a math test where the numbers kept changing position, trying to kick my ass. I had two main goals on this test day--first to survive without getting beaten too badly, and second to impress my master with a succession of kicks and punches.

I used the same two sequences fortified with a few random moves, alternating one after the other. The rest of the combinations that I knew and had practiced so diligently were somehow erased from my memory. My performance was fair and I was evenly matched. Most importantly I hadn't experienced a big defeat. Mike, the boy I was up against in the second round, was older but barely reached my shoulders. He was my biggest obstacle. Not only had he had his Green Belt for over six months, but he was also faster and more flexible than me. I lost my concentration for one split second and BANG, he kicked my head. I shook myself out of shock and responded immediately with two punches to his belly and Mae-Geri, a front kick. The kick I threw wasn't as polished as Mike's kick, but still, it had made contact.

I tried to convince myself that overall I had done pretty well. I wasn't willing to admit, even to myself, that perhaps I wasn't yet Green Belt material. After all, I had paid my dues for this belt, through hours of training, self-sacrifice, discipline, and millions of bruises. I had trained for almost a year. I just had to get my Green Belt. I deserved to go on to the next level. I had earned this belt fair and square!

At the end of the day, once all of the testing had concluded, the students gathered around the ring. We were breathing heavily, partly from exertion, and partly because of the sweaty air. The master started to announce the new belt winners. While the names were announced, the family and friends of those being tested seemed the most excited. They whistled, roared and clapped loudly. I, on the other hand, had no one there to cheer me. This was no surprise though, since I hadn't invited anyone. The thought of having to face my friends and family in the event that I failed was too shameful to bear. I told Mom about the test a few weeks beforehand, but because she was so busy, I knew she'd probably forget. However, after seeing all the cheering, I regretted not having invited anyone.

The master continued announcing the names at a snail's pace. Every student whose name was called jumped from his or her seat, ran to the master, bowed in honor, and received a new belt. "Hey, bro, I made it! I'm purple now!" a short, redheaded kid from the youngest age group yelled out, making everyone laugh.

While waiting for my name to be announced, I nervously scratched at my knee like I was trying to remove an invisible stain. I imagined how it would sound when my name was called. I'd jump into the ring, bow to the master and shake his hand the way my father shakes hands. It'd be a handshake that said, "I'm not a kid anymore, but a real Kung Fu fighter!" Then the master would give me my new Green Belt. I'd turn toward the audience and show them my belt while waving it above my head, clutched in both hands. My belt would turn into a huge ceiling fan that would, to everyone's great relief, beat the heat. The spectators would love my gesture. They'd stand and cheer my name. I'd feel like a gold medalist in the Olympics and I'd blow them kisses.

My reverie ended sharply when I realized that the master hadn't announced my name and had already begun calling names from the next age group. What's going on here? It can't be true! Did I fail? Maybe I just missed hearing my name when I wasn't paying attention. That was probably it... No! That's impossible. If I missed hearing my name he'd repeat it. Maybe he just forgot to call me? It must be a mistake!

It wasn't a mistake. I'd failed! A lump inflated in my throat like a hot air balloon; it competed with the one million pound rock that dropped into the pit of my stomach to see which could cause me more pain. It was the end of the world for me. All the effort that I had made since I got promoted to yellow belt this past year was for nothing. I'd never win the Green Belt that I wanted so badly. It was so unfair! Most of the kids in my group passed the test. Some of them had joined the dojo way after I did. Some weren't even as good as I was. I couldn't understand why the master didn't give me my belt.

I tried to calm down. I could always win the belt next time. I took a deep breath. But then I saw my nemesis, Tom, who lived down the block from me. He was a year younger, but still practiced with my age group. Why did this arrogant kid have to pass the test when I failed? Of course, he didn't miss the opportunity to make fun of me in front of the kids while showing off his new belt. "Pay respect to the green, you yellow wimp!" he said. His words stung me like venom. His scornful eyes wore a wicked smile of bestial joy. It wasn't fair! This little bugger had a huge advantage over me - Rafael. Rafael was Tom's older brother. He was a brown belt and he helped Tom, trained him, and cheered him all the way. I had no one. Life was so unfair! I tried to breathe deeply, but all that I could focus on was the blood boiling in my veins, threatening to melt my body.

I wanted to answer Tom, but my stinging eyes and the choking sensation in my throat convinced me to say nothing. The last thing I wanted was to give him another reason to humiliate me in front of the other kids. I fled the club and hurried home. My house was just half a mile downhill from the dojo, but on that day, it seemed like the cruel street ran on forever. The sidewalks stretched as long as they could, just to make me endure a few extra steps of shame. I felt like everyone on the street knew that I was a loser. I didn't get my belt, but I was getting a variety of looks ranging from blame to disappointment and pity. The looks of pity were the worst of all, I could practically hear the people thinking, "I know what happened to you, poor baby."

I avoided walking past anyone as much as I could, but then I saw the "Smiling Tree." This old oak tree, standing at the corner intersection of *The Great General* and *Anonymous Heroes*, must have been over a hundred years old. It got its name because a knot on its trunk looks like a smiling face. But today, it seemed to give me a look of annoyance. "Run away from here quickly, or else they might change the name of my corner to *The Great Failure* and *Anonymous Losers*," it grumbled at me. I had never felt like any tree had ever had a message for me before. Even though I probably imagined it, it seemed unusual behavior for a tree; then again, this was anything but a usual day. I had no idea that it was about to get even weirder.

5 - NEXT WEEK IS ALWAYS A WEEK FROM NOW

"Ehudik, is that you? How was your day at school? Do you have any homework? Don't wait until bedtime to get it done, okay?" Mom, standing in the kitchen, fired her questions at me the second that I stepped into the house. The aroma wafting through the kitchen door hinted that she was schnitzeling. Usually, I couldn't resist tasting her delicious fried chicken breast, but today I was too upset. I was disappointed that she didn't even remember that it was my test day. However, after considering the questioning she'd have put me through had she remembered that, I became relieved that she forgot.

If she had asked me about the test, I'd have to admit I failed. Then, she'd probably try to comfort me. She might have said, with her heavy Polish accent, something like: "It's okay Ehudik. For me you're always number one. I'm sure you'll do better next time, sweetie." Her lame attempt to cheer me up would leave me feeling even worse. I'd look down at my feet quietly while she continued, "Why do you need all this Karate nonsense anyway? You can hurt yourself there. For a smart kid like you, it's better to stay home and read a good book or do some homework."

"Kung Fu, Mom! Kung Fu! Not Karate!" I'd yell at her, my palms clenched into tight fists. I don't know what would be more annoying, the fact that she called my Kung Fu, "Karate," or the weird way she pronounced the "w" when she said "homework."

I once overheard her telling Dad, "Dr. Gale thinks that Ehud is substituting self pity and lack of confidence with anger, which he directs toward others." I guess Dr. Gale was right, and these "others" were usually my mom. "Unfortunately for him," she had added in a melancholic voice, "he'll only be able to see that when he has kids of his own."

May, my loyal yellow Labrador, who was most skillful at sniffing out my moods from a million miles away, immediately recognized my distress. She unwillingly left her place on the kitchen floor, close to the schnitzels, and raced to my side, catching me by the living room door.

I snuck a glance around the room to confirm that Dad, of course, wasn't home yet. He was the chairman of a company. Alisa, my younger sister, once said to me, "There must be lots of chairs where Dad works; otherwise he wouldn't be coming home so late from work all of the time." She is so adorable.

When I was much younger, Dad used to have a different job. He wasn't as busy as now and we used to play together often. I loved it when he'd throw me in the air with his muscular hands; then Mom would call out, "Put the kid down now! If you drop him, you're dead!" He'd smile in response, revealing two lines of the whitest teeth I've ever seen. His blue eyes shined while he winked mischievously at me. In those days he seemed so big and strong, now he just seems distant and tired.

Since Dad got his new job, I hardly ever saw him anymore. Every morning he left for work before the sun rises, long before I woke up for school. If he came home before I was asleep, it was usually late and I was in my "wind down" mode. He'd say things like, "Hey kid, give me five," while holding out his hand. I'd slap him five and then he'd fling himself down onto the reddish couch in our living room. That would mark the end of our interaction for the day. His next move was usually to try reading the paper; this never lasts long and, soon enough, his loud snoring let us all know he was fallen asleep.

I didn't understand adults. They believed that making a million dollars is important to ensure happiness, but they didn't even have time to be happy. Dad often said, "Family is the most important thing in my life. There's nothing that makes me happier than you guys." But he never spent any time with us. I'd give up all the toys in the world. I'd even donate my new gaming console, which makes me so popular among my friends, if he'd only take me a soccer game some weekend like the other dads. But if he ever did take me to a game, I bet he'd be so tired he'd probably sleep through it.

He was, for sure, not interested in a belt of any color, green or otherwise. A few weeks back he promised me, "Ehudi, next week I'll come home early, and we'll go to a movie or to the beach." But "next week" was always a week from now, and spending time with him has remained just a dream.

Recently too, he replaced talking with shouting. Mom says it's because of the stress at work. "Ehud, stop running in the house!" he screamed at me last Monday. "Ehud, can't you listen to music without sharing it with the entire neighborhood?" he complained over the weekend. "Ehud, how many times have I asked you not to play ball in the house! You'll break something. If you break Grandma's vase, it will break your mother's heart. It's the only memory she has left of her own mother," he yelled two days ago. Why did he care anyway? He also shouted at Mom more than he talked to her. And why were memories from the past more important than having fun right now? You couldn't expect an adult to understand that there's no greater fun than playing ball in the living room. So what if it meant a broken old vase? We could always buy a new one.

From the living room I went into the hallway, May loyally trotted along beside me. When I passed Alisa's room, I didn't even look in. My baby sister was probably playing inside. She wasn't interested in Kung Fu or belts. All she had on her mind were her toys. She was still too young to understand the world she was stuck living in. In her world, each day was a celebration. Every afternoon, she'd sit and play with her dolls and a friend or two. They'd drink imaginary coffee from small plastic cups and eat imaginary cakes. They'd stop talking and giggling only long enough to take another pretend sip or bite.

I wasn't a five-year-old kid like her anymore. Twelve and three quarters was a strange age. I was still a kid, but almost of Bar-Mitzva age. Everything in my life seemed like it was "in between." My voice couldn't even decide whether it should be high pitched, childish like a bird's, or low and deep, like a bear's. Recently, it'd change in the middle of a sentence causing people to laugh at me.

Sometimes I wished I was young like Alisa. I'd like to play all day, have no responsibilities, and no homework. Other times I wished I could be an adult, staying up late and sitting with Mom and Dad's guests at grown-up dinner parties. I liked to listen to the adult's conversations. Sometimes when their friends came over, I raised my chin in a dignified manner and spoke in my most grown-up voice. Then Mom proudly said something like, "Look how he grew up so quickly to be a real man. Soon he'll be ready to leave the nest and fly away." Then I puffed out my chest importantly and flashed my brightest smile.

I slid into my room at the end of the hallway, like a ghost. May quickly snuck in behind me before I shut the door. I flopped down on my bed and she tiptoed toward me to put her head on my knee. She dropped her ears and stared at me with her chocolate eyes. Her sweet look, paired with her wet kisses on my hand, slowly melted my harsh emotions. Dogs like May are God's messengers. They're angels who come from heaven to spread love to the world.

I was starting to relax, when one look into her droopy and glossy eyes reminded me how much I wanted to cry. I wouldn't let myself cry. Two years ago, in front of all of my friends, Rafael told his brother, Tom, "Look at Ehud, doesn't he look like an owl? Let's call him Owly." One tiny tear surfed down my cheek, searching for my lips. They, of course, spotted it and made fun of me. "Owly's a crybaby, Owly's a crybaby," they mocked.

ONE-LEGGED SEAGULL

It was that day when I vowed never to cry again. Since then I haven't been able to cry. I didn't even cry at Grandpa's funeral, my best friend in the whole world besides May. On the day of his funeral, everyone around me was crying, but my tear ducts wouldn't surrender. I was like the spring that we visited on our school trip last year. It was called "The Spring," but there was no water there. The guide explained that there had been a spring there once, but it had dried up forever ago because of changes in the ground structure. Now here I was in my room, less than one hour after my total failure at the test. The tension in my neck was making my throat ache, I was having trouble swallowing because of the lump lodged in my throat, but I couldn't cry because my spring of tears was all dried up.

I decided to take May for a walk in the park to help get my mind off my troubles. Maybe the chilly air of the late afternoon could cool my heated emotions. I grabbed her leash, told Mom we were going to the park, and we headed out. We ran all four blocks. May was in the lead, stopping from time to time to check that I was still following her.

At the park's entrance I put her leash on. The sun was going down fast, and I was glad we reached the park before it had set completely. A few birds battled over some seeds and breadcrumbs scattered on the ground by the water fountain. The flowers drooped after their long, hot day in the sun. A baby began to shriek as its mother pushed the stroller away. I felt a bitter taste in my mouth.

Suddenly May jumped, excited about a ball that rolled past us. She scooped it up in her mouth and it seemed to disappear. A small group of kids, around Alisa's age, surrounded us and angrily demanded that May return their ball. May thought keeping it was a better idea. "Drop it!" I ordered. She did. I patted her head, and dragged her away from the ball.

She was reluctant for a second, dropping her head and letting me know she was disappointed in my decision to leave the ball behind, but then her tail started wagging again and she took the lead as we circled around the park's pond. We walked on the grass between the tall pine trees and the lampposts. May dragged me behind her, sniffing every bush and tree like a detective working on a new murder case. When I grew tired, I chose a spot on a bench that faced the pond. The sun was finishing its descent behind my back, leaving behind a blood-red sky.

May lay beside the bench, her tongue hanging out of her mouth. She looked at me with a sad expression which I read as, "It's a big disaster! You disappointed me today with your failure!" I shifted my eyes away, hung my head and stared at the ground.

"You didn't disappoint her. She's sad only because you're unhappy," said a strange voice from the other side of the bench. It startled me and I jumped to my feet in surprise.

6 - WHAT'S WRONG WITH MY ATTITUDE?

Someone had joined me on the bench while I was focused on May. How could I not notice something like that? In a flash, I leapt to my feet in a Kung Fu grasshopper stance, hopping into an attack position. I clenched my hands into fists and let out a *whoop*. Even if there was no danger, I was ready to defend May and myself. An elderly, bald man with a white and black beard was seated on the other end of my bench, staring at me through round, golden eyeglasses. He scratched the back of his head with his right hand, and rested his left hand on a big potbelly. His belly looked almost as big as my mom's when she was pregnant with Alisa. He was definitely not the scariest person on earth, but Mom always said, "The innocent looking strangers are the most dangerous ones. Don't you ever dare take sweets or anything else from a stranger." I didn't plan to take any risks with this guy.

"Who are you? When did you join me on the bench? How do you know what May thinks? How do you know what I think? Are you a kidnapper?" I threw a million questions at him, all at once. I was buying some time, trying to distract him while I calculated my escape options. Should I flee? Attack? Shout? And what about May? How come she didn't even approach him when he first snuck up on us? May was relaxing on the ground, her head between her front legs. Her eyes looked at me inquiringly, trying to figure out whether my jump meant that I wanted to play or if it had nothing at all to do with her.

My attack position and the questions that followed seemed to surprise the stranger. He retreated, sliding back to the far edge of the bench. He slowly raised his open palm toward me, signaling *STOP*. I froze and waited, alert for his next move. Carefully, he stood up from the bench. His movements were almost in slow motion. Then he approached me, very cautiously, and extended an unsteady hand in greeting. "Simon Master, at your service. When you approached the bench and sat down you were so deep in thought you didn't notice that I was already here."

I wasn't sure I believed his story. How come I hadn't seen him earlier? Had I really been so caught up in my own thoughts so as not to notice this old man? "Do you know that lying is a bad thing?" I asked, while shaking the tip of his fingers with my arm fully extended in order to keep a safe distance. I know it wasn't the most brilliant question to ask, but it was the only one I could come up with on such short notice.

He nodded and surprised me with a smile like none I had ever seen before. It was the kind of smile that felt like it could make me feel that everything would be alright, even if I were being chased through the jungle by hungry cannibals.

I relaxed my balled-up fists slightly. "Are you a Kung Fu master by any chance?" I asked hopefully.

His smile widened and I saw a curious look in his eyes. "No, I'm not that kind of a master. That's my name, Simon Master. Master is my last name."

The balloon of hope that I had inflated just popped, but I had more questions. I didn't completely trust him, but my curiosity outweighed my worries. "How did you know that I thought that I disappointed May? Are you a mind reader?"

He put his left hand gently on my shoulder while offering May a biscuit with his right. "I'm a Tiberiaser, not a mind reader. We Tiberiasers can really feel people. Plus, since retiring, I've been spending two to three hours a day on this very same bench. I watch people and sometimes talk to them. My ability to read body language keeps improving. If you try it for a while, you'll be able to do the same."

"And a Tiberiaser is?"

"Someone who was born and raised in Tiberias, the great city by the Sea of Galilee."

"Oh, Tiberias. We have a school trip there next fall," I said. "So you know how to read body language?" I no longer worried that he planned to harm me, but what he said didn't make sense. Was it possible to read thoughts from body language? "How did you know what May was thinking? How did you know she's only sad because I'm unhappy?" I continued my investigation. Dad used to say, "Your mom could be an FBI interrogator with all of her questions." I guess I knew where I had picked up that trait.

"Thirty years of working as a vet taught me how to read animals better than people. Animals don't try to hide their thoughts. A dog would never lie or disguise its feelings." He smiled at May who licked his hand devotedly.

Strange, I thought, *she usually gets bored with strangers really fast.* "I guess you can't help me," I said quietly.

He returned to his seat on the bench. "Help you with what? I'm not sure what you mean."

"When you said your name, I thought that maybe you were a mysterious Kung Fu master who came from far away to support me. I had a rough day. I failed my Green Belt test. It's a big disaster for me. I trained for a whole year for this test. Now I guess I'll quit the training. I'll never be a Green Belter."

"I'm sorry to hear that. But it doesn't sound like such a big disaster. I failed many times in my long life, but eventually I learned never to give up. I learned to keep trying until I succeeded."

"I'm not sure I have the energy to try again. I'm giving up."

"But if you don't try, you'll never win."

"I know that," I snapped. This guy was starting to get on my nerves. "But no matter how hard I try, I can't win. If I had a big brother to help me, like Rafael who helps Tom, I'd have a chance. Without help, it's too hard for me." I knelt down next to May and started to dig a hole in the dirt.

"Help? Everyone needs help these days. What kind of help are you looking for?"

"I could use the help of Cinderella's fairy godmother. Maybe the stardust that turned a pumpkin into a carriage could turn my yellow belt to green, and also turn me from a loser into a fierce Kung Fu warrior," I joked sadly while pretending to sprinkle stardust on my head.

His right palm supported his lower back. "I'm neither a fairy godmother, nor a Kung Fu master. At my age, my power is in my experience, not in my body. I know how you feel though. I too could use help sometimes."

"What kind of help could someone like you need?" I asked. I didn't care much, but if I could find a way to help him, maybe he could help me.

"Many things. Only yesterday, I had a computer problem. My son and grandson live across the ocean in America. I tried to send them a letter through the modem, but the screen couldn't find a page."

I raised my left eyebrow. "Do you mean you tried to email them but you couldn't login into your webmail page?"

He too raised his own left eyebrow. "Yes. Isn't that what I said?"

"That's so easy. I could teach you in less than ten minutes."

He sighed. "That would be very nice of you. You seem like a good boy. You remind me of my grandson. You and he are about the same age. I miss him so much. America is far. Sometimes he emails me pictures, but it's always difficult for me to get them to open. I'd really appreciate any help that you could give me with that." He smiled sheepishly. "How could I return the favor?"

Excellent question, I thought, as a group of kids ran past. He said that his power is in his experience; this probably dates back to the time when the Dead Sea was just a little bit sick. *How can he help me?* "Did you serve in the army? Did you learn how to fight?"

He poked his index finger against his forehead. I do the same thing when I have no good answers. "I did serve in the army, but many years ago. I even trained in Kung Fu when I was your age. However, in order to win this belt, you'll need a real master, not a retiree like me."

I was ready to give up on him. This old man seemed useless. But, at the moment, he was my only option. A voice deep inside told me that this Tiberiaser would have more to offer than I could see. It couldn't be coincidental that we just happened to both sit on the same bench. I imagined Simon Master was really the big brother of Master Yoda. It was possible that he could be a weird Jedi Master who looked helpless, but had actually come to test me... to see if I deserved his training.

"You know," he said hesitating, after a long pause, "my favorite of Hazal's sayings is, 'I have learned from all of my teachers - by teaching, you learn yourself.' These ancient Jewish sages have some great messages. Although I can't train you in Kung Fu, if you help me with my computer, I can share some things with you from my life experience. I'm sure I have a lot to teach and a lot to learn."

"I guess you're right," I said reluctantly, finding it hard to hide my disappointment. But, I still couldn't let go of the idea of making him my private Kung Fu master. "My master told us that Chinese monks developed the art of Kung Fu after observing the fighting movements and strategies of animals. Each animal uses its individual advantages to cover its disadvantages. The white crane uses its fragile appearance and powerful wings, the tiger uses its strength and deadly claws, and the monkey uses its shrewdness and agility. You said that you used to be a vet; I bet you worked with lots of different animals. Maybe you could use your experience to show me how to become a better fighter."

He laughed loudly at this comment, and his laughter ended abruptly with a short, dry cough. "I healed animals. I didn't watch them fight. I like your persistence though, kid. Unfortunately, there's no way I could teach you Kung Fu. But I do think I can help you with your attitude."

"Attitude? What's wrong with my attitude?"

"Well you said that you want to become a better fighter, but then you also told me that it was Chinese monks who developed the art of Kung Fu. Kung Fu is an art, not a fight. Every Bruce Lee fan knows that." He winked. "My life experience has taught me that in order to improve in any art form, you need to be an artist, not a fighter."

"I understand," I said, but I wasn't sure that I really did. "Can you please explain what you mean by---" a children's TV show tune interrupted my question mid-sentence. I couldn't remember which show it was from. I looked around trying to find the source of the music.

"It's me," Simon said, while pulling a cell phone from his pocket and checking the screen. "It's my ringtone alarm for supper. I can't see without my reading glasses, but it's probably six-thirty already. I'm sorry young man, but I have to run. We can continue our nice chat tomorrow. Dinner is served at seven p.m. sharp at the retirement home. If I don't make it on time, evil Alfred will steal my seat at the table next to beautiful Mary. We don't want that to happen, do we?" He jumped off the bench as light-footed as a young man. He waved goodbye while taking big steps toward the south exit of the park.

"Ehud, my name is Ehud." I called out after him from the bench, hoping he could hear me. I watched him head out of the park. Even though in a hurry, he still stopped every now and again to smell a flower or pet a dog.

'The name is Master. Simon Master.' I envisioned a younger version of Simon, sporting a James Bond suit and introducing himself. He was really something this guy. On the one hand he quoted ancient sages, knew that "Kung Fu is an art, not a fight," and had lots of experience; on the other hand he had a kid's ringtone, and was just an old Tiberiaser who, apparently, raced someone called Evil Alfred for a seat at the dinner table. He couldn't teach me how to fight. *Was he the help I was looking for?* I looked at May, "What do you think, girl? Maybe he's an angel that came to help me. What do I have to lose?" May barked once and gave me the same look as when she agrees to obey a command. I smiled. "I knew you'd agree."

On our way home I thought about what Simon had said. "I can help you with your attitude... Kung Fu is an art, not a fight... in order to improve in any art form, you need to be an artist, not a fighter." I had never thought about Kung Fu like this. I did perceive training and the test as a kind of struggle. Truth be told, I was sort of fighting against it. I wondered if a different attitude could bring different results. The more I considered Simon's words about being an artist and not a fighter, the more my anticipation for our next meeting grew. I was glad that I had met Simon, and new hope pushed my earlier shame and disappointment away. I decided that going to meet Simon first thing the next morning would be the best first step toward winning my Green Belt.

7 - THE GENIE FELL ASLEEP

I didn't sleep well throughout the night. I was too excited thinking about my morning meeting with Simon. Finally I had someone to help me, like a big brother who could share his experiences with me. God hadn't answered my prayers quite the way I had expected, but still, he had answered. *I'm going to be a Kung Fu fighter... I mean a Kung Fu artist.* I quickly revised my thoughts, just in case Simon could read them. I didn't want him to change his mind and decide not to help me because of my attitude.

Excitement lost to fatigue and I started to doze off. Before I had a chance to fall asleep, I was pulled out of the dream world by a loud whisper coming from Alisa's room. "Ehud! Ehud! The genie fell asleep." At first I was not sure if I had imagined hearing that, but then I heard her calling again. I rolled out of my bed and zombie-walked my way to her room. It was so dark that I bumped into every possible obstacle on my way to her room. I found her curled up against the wall in her bed. She was shivering and hugging her teddy bear tightly. "The genie, it fell asleep and there is no one to protect me from bad dreams," she whispered, so softly I could barely hear her.

"Don't worry, I'll wake him in a flash." I crouched down and looked under her bed. "Genie... Hey, Mr. Genie... wake up!" I whispered into the empty space. "You need to protect Ali from bad dreams." I waited for a few seconds. "It's okay, he's awake now." I smiled at Alisa as I stood up again. It had been my idea to make up the story about the genie living under her bed. It was brilliant, and had saved me many late-night trips to her room. Thanks to this genie, she rarely felt the need to wake me in the middle of the night when she suspected the onset of nightmares.

"Thanks. You're a great brother. I'm lucky to have you and the genie to keep me safe," she said, and a yawn stretched across her freckled face.

"Sure. That's what big brothers and genies are for. Good night Ali. Sweet dreams."

"Now that the genie is awake again, I'll be fine. Good night, Ehudi." She blew me an air-kiss.

* * * * *

"Ouch!" On my way back to bed, I stepped on a wooden toy soldier. This soldier, which was laying in wait to ambush whatever may have been lurking in the dark, dug right into my bare foot. There was a cry of pain, and I was unsure whether it had come from him or from me. The fact that I had even wondered about the source of the noise was sufficient proof that I was ready for a good sleep. I hadn't played with my toy soldiers for years; Alisa or May must have borrowed one and forgotten to put it back in my toy box.

When I was younger, I spent hours creating imaginary worlds with toys that Dad had carved for me. I'd strategically place soldiers, tanks and airplanes on the carpet. Once these little worlds were ready, I, myself, would transform into a raging God. I began many world wars, and I always let the good guys kick ass. All the bad soldiers would die and the good ones would win a painful victory. The only thing that had the power to temporarily save my little worlds from the ravages of war was Mom. Sometimes she'd call me for lunch just as a war was about to erupt, then my world would gain a few more merciful minutes. However, right after lunch, it'd be extinguished. There's nothing like a good toy war for dessert. I picked up the toy soldier and put him back in the toy box. I jumped into my bed and immediately entered into the world of dreams.

* * * * *

Warriors and artists with different color belts practiced their maneuvers all across my dreams. They all wore Kung Fu suits. Even Grandma, who died many years ago, was there in a white suit and pink belt. She was standing proud and tall. She looked exactly like I remembered her from old pictures, before she got sick and passed away. She was conducting an orchestra of half naked cannibals who practiced katas with soup pots on their heads. She used a spoon and a carrot instead of the typical conductor's baton.

I was walking on a long, yellow brick road. I saw fights breaking out everywhere. Good vs. evil, white suits vs. black suits, Green Belts vs. brown belts. It was like one of those Bruce Lee movies. The journey continued and the people around began to disappear, one by one, until I was alone. A tree appeared from out of the dark, then a second one, then a million more – it became an endless forest. A pair of evil, green eyes peered at me from between the trees. I jumped into a battle position, roared and... fled as fast as I could. Unfortunately "as fast as I could," was as fast as a lazy snail. I'm a fast runner, and usually I win every race against my classmates, but this time my feet felt like they were being held down by an invisible creature. I looked back. A large tiger with green stripes that had Tom's face was chasing me. I tried to run faster, but he was closing the distance quickly. I could feel his warm breath on my neck and I imagined his sharp claws tearing through my back.

* * * * *

I decided that this was too much and I woke myself from the dream. Being able to wake myself from nightmares had already saved me from several dream–death experiences. The excitement of having escaped the tiger was exhausting. I drifted back to sleep, but this time it was dreamless.

The next morning, despite my restless night, I jumped out of bed opting to skip my usual ritual of nestling under the soft blanket for a few more minutes. I slapped together a sandwich to take with me and ran with May to the park to meet with Simon. I completely forgot this was a school day.

Luckily, Mom took Alisa to preschool before I even left the house. She wouldn't have understood the importance of this meeting with Simon anyway. She knew nothing about Kung Fu as an art. For her art was only the stuff in museums or art galleries. She couldn't understand how a bunch of kids in white suits, practicing animal fight moves, could be considered an art form. As far as I could tell, for her, this was all just an excuse to avoid doing homework.

I entered the park and started playing Frisbee with May, while waiting for Simon to arrive. One hour passed, then another one; still, he didn't show up. I sat down, ate my sandwich, stood up, sat down again, crossed my right leg over my left, crossed my left leg over my right. I walked around the bench, I lay on the grass, I closed my eyes, I opened my eyes. I whistled, I sang, I cursed, I jumped on one leg, then on two. But still, he didn't show up.

Any other kid would've given up long before. Another kid would've gone home with his tail between his legs, but not me. Like Mom loved to say, "Ehudik was born in May. He's a Taurus. Taurus people as you know, are very stubborn." I think she's wrong. As a young kid I used to be stubborn like those pistachios you can never open; however, as I grew up, I progressed from being stubborn to being firm. I'd wait as long as it took until Simon appeared.

A few of May's dog friends came to the park with their owners. I scanned the park to make sure that there weren't any park rangers around, and let her off the leash to play with her friends. After about an hour all the dogs had left and gone back to their homes. I looked around the relatively deserted park. It wouldn't be crowded until school let out for the day. Fortunately, this was one of the colder days of the season. Yesterday's scorching weather had ceded to the cheerful west wind, which was fortified by the sea's energy. The wind toyed with the few people who walked through the park. It stroked their faces and tried to steal their hats.

Unfortunately, Simon wasn't one of those people. *Where is he?* I repeatedly asked myself. I felt stupid. I had been so excited to have met Simon yesterday that I forgot to ask where and when we were to meet again. Was he planning to come at all? If so, what time? And where? I squeezed my fists and released a growl like that of wounded prey.

Another hour passed. I started to question whether or not he was real. Maybe I had just imagined him. How could he just appear next to me on the bench like a phantom in a dream? Doubt snuck into my mind, like the burglar who snuck into our neighbor's house last month. I started to think about our meeting. If he was real, how come May hadn't reacted when we approached him? She loved people. She was always a too-friendly jumper. She had never been shy before, even with someone she had just met for the first time. Maybe I had just fallen asleep on the bench and dreamt him up, like I had with Grandma and the tiger.

I knew I should leave. There was no point in waiting. I got angry. *Why isn't he coming?* I did a quick scan of the park. *Why did everything around have to be so green, like the belt I didn't win?* I decided to just go home, but in my head, I kept hearing the echo of Alisa's words from the night before, "You're a great brother. I'm lucky to have you and the genie to keep me safe." She was lucky. I didn't have a big brother or a genie to protect or guide me. I changed my mind about leaving, I wasn't willing to give up the hope that I may have just found my own guide. I had to stay.

I lowered myself to the grass and lay on my belly. After a while, I closed my eyes and hit the ground with my fists. Self-pity enveloped me like a sleeping bag, blocking any other emotion. One more hour passed. I wavered; I tried to convince myself that Simon wasn't the perfect guide for me anyway. May, tired from chasing the squirrels, decided to give them a break and came to sit in front of me.

"Home, let's go home, yes, home, let's go," she signaled to me with her eyes and nose. I picked up her leash, led her to the shade of the pine trees and ordered her to lie down. I lay down there as well and rested my head on her belly. I scratched above my ear and tried to concentrate. Maybe he had forgotten to come. Maybe he had totally forgotten me. Older people do become senile. Even Mom, who is way younger than Simon, was always looking for something. "Where the hell did I put my keys? Did anyone see my eyeglasses? Ehud, did you, by any chance, take the book I left on the table?" Later, when she found whatever she had lost, she'd sigh deeply and say, "The years are creeping up on me and stealing my memory."

A while later, my stomach felt like a vacuum. It signaled to my brain that it was time to eat. I had hardly eaten all day. Thinking about food shifted my thoughts away from Simon. I decided that a piece of cake with ice cream would make me feel better. I took May's leash and we started to walk home.

While walking and fantasizing about the dessert I was about to enjoy, questions started to fill my head: *What did he say yesterday? How many hours did he spend in the park? Which hours of the day did he visit? What time was it when we met?* I'm so stupid! He had said, "I've been spending two to three hours a day on this very same bench." He left at 6:30 sharp. This means he shouldn't be here before 3:30. I looked at the sun, high up in the sky. It was toward the far side of the park, slowly sailing behind a cloud. Yesterday the sunset was behind us, which means I'm on the wrong side of the pond. May had pulled me in every possible direction yesterday, confusing me. Eventually I had ended up on the far side of the park, where I met him.

An excitement grew in my chest and desperation made some room for hope. "May, leave this Golden Retriever's butt alone, we have to go back to the other side of the park," I said. It was quarter to four and if I was lucky, Simon was already waiting for me on our bench.

8 - THE WIN IS TREASURED IN THE ACT OF SURRENDERING

I crossed the park to the other side of the pond and found the right bench. It was empty. I circled around the area, visually searching over the short hills and wild bushes. When I had almost finished a full loop, I heard a familiar voice behind me, "Hey Ehud, it's good to see you again. I was just thinking of you."

I was stricken by a mixture of joy and surprise. *My new friend was here! He even remembered my name.* I turned to face him with the widest smile my cheeks would allow. "I thought that you disappeared. I was worried that you forgot about me or that I just imagined meeting you."

"No, you didn't imagine me, and of course I didn't forget you. Thank God, I'm not senile yet." Pleasant words accompanied his calming smile.

I quickly summarized for him the awful morning I had experienced.

He took a seat on the bench and invited me to join him. "I believe that I unintentionally delivered a lesson to you this morning," he said. "The win is treasured in the act of surrendering."

"I don't get it. What do you mean that you delivered a lesson? Firstly, you weren't even here, and secondly, how can surrendering lead to a win? If you surrender, you lose." I was glad I finally found him, but he sounded like a confused, elderly man. If my dad could have heard him talk like this, he'd laugh. Then with an enigmatic smile, he'd probably tell Simon something like, "You're totally drunk, dude."

"The whole morning your attention was fixed on the desire to meet me. And that was exactly what you experienced - the desire to meet me," Simon explained. "You even forgot today was a school day. Then due to the despair of your unfulfilled desire, you surrendered and thought about something else. Only then did you ask yourself the obvious questions. Only then did you figure out where and when to meet me."

"So in order to find you, I had to get frustrated?"

"Not necessarily. In this case, you reached surrendering through the frustration. Instead, you could choose to surrender. You can give up the desire without first experiencing the frustration. Then you can think more clearly. Surrendering can be reached either deliberately or through suffering and despair."

"I'm still not totally sure I understand you. You are basically saying that I should always give up my dreams and accept my failure? Be a loser?" I asked, my left eye squinting in disagreement.

"Surrendering is not giving up. Never give up unless you choose to. Surrendering is the opposite of resisting, it's becoming one with the flow of life."

I sighed and put my hands on my hips in annoyance.

"I can see that you have lots of questions," he said. "That makes sense. It's a tricky concept to understand. In school, they don't teach you to let go of your resistances. However, you have more answers than you think. A real Tiberiaser allows every ROWer to find his own answers. Take your---"

"ROWer?"

"Someone who lives in the Rest of the World, not in Tiberia." He grinned. "Take your time. Think a bit about what I said. Find your own answers. I must run now. I have a yoga class before dinner. Mary is saving me a spot in the first row, right in front of the instructor. If I don't make it on time, Alfred will steal my spot, or find a prank to pull on me. I've known this guy since our preschool days, and he has the nerve to say to me, 'Simon, my dear friend, in love and war there are no rules.' Believe me, with friends like him who needs enemies?" He turned around, hurried off and gave me a quick wave.

It had been another short meeting which brought more questions than answers. He was right about at least one thing, the pressure to meet him had affected my thinking. Releasing this pressure could only help. I still wasn't sure how much I could learn from this man who was always rushing off to another place. Yet, I had no other choice. I decided to ask him to explain his idea about surrendering more clearly at our next meeting. Then I could decide if he was any good.

9 - EVERY NOTHING IS SOMETHING

I knew I'd get in trouble with Mom for skipping school, so when Dad came home I took advantage of how tired he was. I had him sign a piece of paper saying I was sick. As I expected, he didn't even look at it. I went to my room and lay on my back, staring at the glow-in-the-dark stars on my bedroom ceiling. I thought about what Simon had said. *Surrender. Surrender, but don't give up.* What did he mean? I wasn't sure what exhausted me more - my restless night, the long wait in the park, or the thoughts about surrendering. Whatever the reason, I fell asleep immediately.

* * * * *

I'm on a school trip in the north of Israel. My whole class is canoeing on the calm water of the Jordan River. Suddenly the sun disappears, kidnapped by a group of reckless clouds. A malicious wind disrupts the peacefulness, and the current of the river starts to flow with great force. I look around, my classmates have all vanished. They left me all alone on the wild river. I try to call to them, but my voice can't be heard over the sound of the blowing wind and the rushing water. I fight the giant waves and the forceful current with franticly rowing hands, trying to navigate safely to shore, but the river is stronger than me. Tree branches hanging above the river scratch my arms and face. The big rocks underneath the water hit the canoe mercilessly, threatening to smash it. My backside is heavily bruised. Fighting against the flow is exhausting; I'm lost and out of control. Is this my end? Am I going to drown? Wait a second, what about Simon? Where is he?

"Surrender!" I hear his voice coming from a distance, carried by the wind. What? Surrender now? This isn't the time to surrender, this is the time to fight. I'm being violently carried away; if I don't fight, I'll die. He must have lost his mind. "Surrendering is becoming one with the flow of life..." I hear his soothing voice again. I continue to struggle, but I'm losing my strength quickly. For lack of any other option, I decide to try his advice. I try to relax in the canoe. I stop struggling and surrender to the flow. Using the paddle, I adjust the canoe carefully between the waves. My muscles loosen and my exhaustion disappears. To my surprise, I enjoy the rushing current and the cool wind that blows against my face. The river no longer seems so dangerous. I try to maneuver the canoe to avoid hitting rocks and branches. If I can see them from far enough away, it becomes easy to redirect the canoe. It's like a game that I'm getting really good at playing. I'm not drifting aimlessly anymore, I'm flowing with direction. Slowly I steer the canoe from the center of the river to the bank. I spot a strong branch extending far out over the river. I grab it and pull myself onto land. I'm saved!

* * * * *

I awoke from the dream. The sun was already peeking through the window. It too had just risen, stretching its early morning rays after its own long night's sleep. Instead of jumping out of bed like I had the day before, I closed my eyes and fell back asleep. After yesterday's frustration, it was better to be patient.

ONE-LEGGED SEAGULL

* * * * *

Much later, after the school day was over, I sat on our bench, watching May chase her tail. She always came so close to catching it but she never could.

"How are you doing?" I started the conversation with Simon, who had just sat down. "How was your yoga class?"

"It was good, thanks for asking. I'm working on my flexibility and improving it. Every artist needs to practice in order to stay on the artist's path. Yoga keeps my body flexible, and the meetings I have with you keep my mind flexible. Oh, I was thinking, we need to schedule a time when you can come to visit me in the retirement home. You promised to teach me how to send emails, remember?"

"Sure, I told you it's not a problem. Just say when."

"Great, we'll set something up for next week. I want to send a letter to my grandson. So, what's new in your world?"

I told him about the dream I had. "I understand the dream, but I don't know how to apply it to my real life."

"What do you understand?" he asked.

"I understand the difference between drifting and flowing. The direction was the same, I had no choice. The river was much stronger than me. The difference was in my feeling. I noticed that once I let go of the stress and stopped struggling against being carried away, I was able to calm down and change the situation. You know what? Just by saying out loud what happened, I already understand my dream even more so than before."

"Very good. You found out that surrendering means letting go of the stress. It's releasing your attachment to a specific target at a specific time, no matter what."

"So, I shouldn't set goals in my life?" I asked, surprised.

"That's a good question. Goals can either be helpful or impeding."

"How so?"

"Without goals, you wander with no direction, you can't progress. But getting attached to achieving your goals can make you blind to other opportunities and frustrate you."

"Hmmm. So what can I do?"

"There are many things you can do. My way is to set a goal, and then set a direction that will help to achieve it. Then I release my attachment to the results, focus on the path, and take actions that progress me."

A group of loud kids crowded the walkway in front of us. They blocked the way for a cyclist coming from the other direction. "And what happens if the path is blocked?" I asked, looking at the guy who had to stop and wait for the kids to clear the road.

"I always keep my direction in mind. If the path is blocked, I have many options. I can wait like the biker you're watching, I can pick another path, or I can ask whoever blocks it to move. Surrendering is accepting whatever comes my way, releasing any resistance, and then continuing moving on in the direction I set."

"So far, I think I get it," I said. "Do you maybe have some more examples? It's still confusing."

"When did you last get a vaccine?"

"About two months ago in school, why?"

"How was it?"

"A nightmare."

"Let me guess," he said, "the shot itself wasn't that painful. You suffered more from fear and resistance. If you'd have surrendered to the fear of the shot, you'd have had to deal with just the pain. Then it wouldn't have been 'a nightmare,' as you called it. The resistance itself caused more suffering than the object of your resistance."

Remembering, I rubbed my shoulder in the place where I got the injection. "You're right, it really wasn't so bad. But when I saw the needle, I was so afraid that I almost fainted. The school nurse had to get me a chair and a glass of water before I could go back to class. Hmmm, I think I understand better what you're saying."

He rose. "I'm glad to hear that. I need to do some stretching, my body is a bit sore from class yesterday." He bent over and touched the ground with both palms while keeping his legs straight. Then he stretched his back.

"Not bad," I said.

Simon returned to the bench grinning. "Enough showing off, let's look at what happened when you gave up waiting for me yesterday. What did you do after you surrendered?"

I waved my hand. "Wait a second. I didn't really surrender; I didn't even know what surrender meant."

He chuckled. "You did it without knowing. It doesn't make a difference if you know you're doing it or not."

"What do ya mean?"

"The only difference is awareness. If you know how to surrender, then you can do it deliberately; otherwise it can happen only after some suffering occurs, like you experienced yesterday."

"Okay, I got that. But how exactly did I surrender?"

"When you felt hungry, you decided that the meeting with me could wait. Suddenly, eating became a priority. That's when you surrendered your need to meet me right away and at any cost. What happened then?"

I chuckled. "I thought about the dessert I was going to have. Wait a second, that made me stop thinking about you, and soon after, all of these questions started to pop up."

"Exactly. Shifting your attention created the surrendering and that's what helped you to find me."

I frowned. "So, you say that surrendering is not giving up, right? Hmmm, I can see that, because I never gave up meeting with you. Then, what you call surrendering happened when I was open to doing something else, and I was willing to wait to meet you another time. Okay, I get it. When I surrendered, I started to think clearly."

A sudden westerly breeze almost stole my baseball cap. I held it in my hand and looked at Simon to see what he had to say. He mussed my hair. "I couldn't have phrased it better myself. The surrendering enabled you to leave your frustration behind and see the situation from another point of view. You accepted the fact that I wasn't there, and got ready to leave. That's how you managed to change the situation. One of the rules I have in my life is, 'if I can change it, I change it; otherwise I accept it.' As the Borg says in *Star Trek*, 'resistance is futile.'"

"How do I know what can be changed and what can't?" I asked.

"You know what? I never thought about it before. Theoretically almost everything can be changed. Even if it takes extra time, effort and courage."

"So do you mean I actually decide what I can change?"

"Sounds like a great insight," he said, and I learned a new word: *insight*.

A young kid started to cry on a nearby bench. "It's not going to help you," the mother said to her son. "You aren't going to get ice cream." The kid continued to cry and the mom looked helpless. Eventually she said, "Okay, one scoop only. But you better eat your dinner when we get home."

Simon laughed. "Young kids test borders all the time. They know what I just told you."

"Right." I smiled. "I've also made mom change her decisions more than once."

"I bet you have. I'm still trying to make changes all the time, but sometimes I decide that I can't change something. It can be because it takes too much effort, or because the situation is clearly out of my control. Then I accept what's happening and see what can be learned from it. I convert the experience into a tool for my growth. I ask myself, 'what can I do to improve myself? What changes can I make in the future?' The only thing I'm giving up is my resistance."

"It sounds like you treat whatever you can't change, like a class that you have to take at school." I surprised myself with an observation that sounded smart.

"You're absolutely right. With every obstacle, I see a class which I forgot that I signed up for. Thanks to that way of thinking, I never get stuck in helpless situations."

"So surrendering is letting go of helplessness, and an unwanted reaction, right?" I made sure I was following him.

"More great insights," he said. "You can surrender to any thought, feeling or event you don't like."

"I think I understand what you are saying, and I think I know someone who follows your rule."

His eyes filled with curiosity. "Who?"

"May," I said. Hearing her name, she looked at me. Then, since she didn't see a treat or a ball in my hands she dropped her head down between her front legs. "Sometimes when May and I go for a walk, I want to go in one direction, and she wants to go in another. She'll plant her paws firmly on the ground, fold her tail, and lower her head and shoulders. She shows me she isn't pleased with my choice. Sometimes I let her take the lead. However, if I'm actually going somewhere specific and she sees that I insist, she rushes in the direction that I have chosen, making sure that she takes the lead. She raises her tail, and I can tell that she is ready for a new adventure, even on a path that she didn't pick herself. She could be upset and spend the rest of the trip angry, but she always chooses to enjoy the trip whether she decided the route or not.

"Excellent example," he said. "May surrenders the attachment to her favorite route and chooses to make the most of what comes next. And while doing this, she never gives up her primary plan, to enjoy the trip. She tries to lead whenever she can, but she doesn't try to force it when she can't. Leading takes second place to her first goal of enjoying the journey."

I proudly petted her back. "She's smarter than I thought. She's a master in surrendering."

"Of course. Dogs are great masters, who do you think taught me all of this?"

"What a waste," I said, scratching my ear in puzzlement. "All this time I had a great master next to me and I didn't even know it. Speaking of great masters, I still can't believe you could teach me the concept of surrendering when you weren't even with me. You're a great teacher, even better than my teacher, Mrs. Gendler… and she has eyes in the back of her head."

He chuckled. "You're funny. See, the reason I could teach you without being present is because every nothing is something."

I opened my eyes wide. "Now that's sounding crazy!"

"Do you see the brick wall on the building in front of us?" he asked, while pointing at a white building outside of the park. "Is it a complete piece? Or are there parts with no bricks?"

"I'm not sure where you're heading with this question, but I think the answer is no. The wall surface isn't one piece; there are windows in it too."

"You're absolutely correct. There are holes in the wall for the windows. The 'missing space' is a window, so the nothing is something. And since a wall with a window is usually worth more than a wall without one, every time you're missing something, you should check to see what 'something' the 'nothing' has created. Surrendering leads to a victory, because the nothing is really something."

"Yessss!" I heard screams coming from a group of kids nearby. I looked in their direction and saw an upset goalie picking up a ball from the net behind him. He slammed it down on the grass and caught it again when it bounced. A few other kids celebrated their goal with high-fives. I turned back to Simon. "I get it with the wall and the windows, but how can I use it in my life?"

"Well, you tell me. What wouldn't have occurred had you actually won the Green Belt the other day?"

I had to think for a minute. "I wouldn't have met you," I said, my eyes widening in surprise. "You mean to say that I wouldn't have learned all of these ideas that you've showed me?"

He just nodded yes.

"So, the nothing, the no belt, became something, the lessons with you, right?" I asked.

He confirmed again, nodding.

"I think I get this. When I waited for you, I resisted waiting. The resistance created unhappiness and made me mad. Now I feel much better; and it's not only because I found you, it's really because the resistance feels like it's gone."

He grinned. "I told you, you've got all the answers."

I shook my head, disbelieving. A heavy gust of wind went through the park, stealing the kids' ball and blowing May's ears up. I looked at the reeds around the pond bowing toward the water, and watched a small branch of an oak tree crack under the pressure of the wind and fall to the ground.

"Did you see that?" I asked Simon, turning my face away from the passing gusts.

"Yeah, that's a strong wind. Can you see the difference between the way the reeds and the oak tree deal with the wind?"

I nodded, "The poor reeds, they bend until they almost reach the water."

"I feel worse for the oak tree."

"I don't get it."

"The reeds choose the total surrendering approach. They bow and wait for the moment they can rise again. The oak is strong, and doesn't move even an inch. But when the pressure is too much, its inability to move becomes a liability, and it can break as we just saw."

"So the reeds are doing things better?"

"Frankly, I think the right balance between the two approaches works best for me. When I need to, I surrender like the reeds and when it's time to be strong, I stand tall like the oak."

"Got it. Balance sounds good. I can understand how the reeds' letting go under pressure can help them to survive a strong wind."

"Do I feel a 'but' coming?" he asked.

"Yes," I said, with a sad expression. "I can't help thinking about Grandpa, how he was so sick. I didn't like to see him suffer like that. I couldn't accept the state that he was in. I couldn't surrender my wish that he'd get healthy again. I think that in a case like that, you can't ever surrender."

"If you can't accept something *outside* of you, like something difficult that happens to another person, accept what is *inside* of you. It's natural to be sad. Accept your pain, accept the grief. Focus on the internal sorrow and not on the situation that caused it. Experience the pain, surrender to it, let go of the resistance to what goes on in that moment, and be released."

"Not sure I see what you're saying. How do I let go of that much pain?"

"By experiencing it fully with no resistance. Give it the space it requires, and breathe into it. Don't try to stop it. Create it deliberately and really feel it. Intensify the feeling as if you really want it, like you invited it, like it's all just a game. Don't be afraid of it, befriend it. If you need to cry, do. If you need to scream, don't hesitate."

I stared at him. "Why should I make a bad feeling bigger?"

"When you have a strong pain, it contains you and you can't see outside of it. While you're enlarging your pain by choice, give it more and more space. Push it toward its edges like you're inflating a balloon. When you reach the edges, you're the one who contains the pain since you can see its edges."

"What edges?"

"All pain occupies a different space in your life. For example, a physical pain sits somewhere in the body, whereas a mental pain can be locked in your memory."

"I see. And how does going to the edges of a pain work to solve the pain?" I asked, doubtfully. "I can barely understand that idea. It sounds pretty impossible."

"Actually this is nature's way of releasing. For example, if a man is caught in an ocean whirlpool, his natural reaction is to resist so he can stay alive. He'll struggle to stay afloat while he's being pulled down. His fight against the ocean will exhaust him until he eventually loses and drowns."

"Ouch. Does he have any chance of surviving?"

"Yes, but he'd have to surrender the fight. He should let the ocean pull him down or even better, deliberately choose to dive down as deep as he can. It's scary, but at the bottom of the whirlpool there is a sort of exit that will propel him out. Since the ocean is stronger, he can only survive the whirlpool by surrendering."

"Sounds scary," I said.

"It is."

"Does it work only with pain and whirlpools?"

"A great question. It works the same with every emotion. Try to surrender to sorrow, happiness, hope, despair, and every other feeling you have. Experience them without resistance until they disappear. Every emotion will pass eventually. Resistance not only magnifies an emotion but it also makes that sensation stay with you longer."

"Wait a second," I said, and paused to watch a butterfly that landed on my thigh. "I can understand why you want to let go of the feeling of being sad, but why would you want to let go of happiness? I want happiness to stay longer. According to what you've just said, if I resist, I can make it stay longer. So, in that case, if I resist, that helps me, right?"

"You have some good questions today. If you're happy and want to hold on too hard to the happiness, then happiness will suddenly change into the fear of losing happiness. The resistance to losing it will ruin all of the fun in your happiness."

"Hmmm. Okay, I think I gotcha."

"Once you have fully experienced one emotion, you're ready to experience the next one. Life will become more fun if it's full of surprises and you have no resistance. You'll flow and not drift."

"It sounds right, I guess. And then bad emotions won't come back anymore?"

"Foul!" one of the soccer players shouted. "No way!" another kid answered angrily. In seconds all the kids had surrounded the first two, everyone shouting at everyone else. But in no time, the whole group was playing again.

Both Simon and I laughed as we watched them.

"Hard emotions start with negative thoughts," Simon explained. "You think how someone has mistreated you and it makes you feel bad. If you don't want these feeling to return, you need to unthink whatever thought created it or deliberately think a happier thought."

"It sounds good, but when I'm really angry and need to do this trick most, I bet I'll be too afraid or confused to try it. How can I give my pain more space, when every cell in my brain is shouting, 'stop it now'?"

"I totally agree about how hard that is. That's why you need to be an artist and practice this with small things. Try to practice every day. Every bus you miss, every test you fail, every time you're wrong or embarrassed, every time you're sick, every time your mother asks if you finished your homework, every time your father shouts at you, every time… just surrender. Let the resistance go, accept everything as it is. Even if it hurts."

I squeezed my eyes, like someone in pain. "Right, it can really hurt. I'm not sure if I should try it."

"As I said, try it on the small events first. Accepting the situation as it is, no matter how difficult, makes at least some of the suffering easier. That's why everything hurts less when you don't resist it."

"But isn't resistance protecting me?" I asked.

"You'd think so, but it isn't. If you accept pain with patience when pain can't be avoided, it won't hurt as much. If you flow instead of drift and fight, you'll be more able to change the situation. You shouldn't face any situation, no matter how intense it seems, with panic." He looked at me with an inquiring look, checking to see if I was still following him.

"You know what? I can see what you're saying. When I didn't surrender, I blocked out lots of choices. I chose one path but missed the rest."

"Exactly. There's always a path that you can take that is less painful. Here is your homework assignment from today's meeting: From now on, view every problem as a chance to practice." He stroked my hair like Grandpa used to. "Accept it with love and be thankful for the chance to train yourself."

"Makes sense. I will." His assignment sounded interesting; at least it wouldn't be boring like the homework from school that was so important to Mom.

"Wonderful. It's almost seven and you know what that means. Yesterday, you-know-who stole the last of the strawberry cupcakes right out of my hands. I had to eat a chocolate one, which I hate.

He's shameless. When we were kids, my mother warned me about this rude boy." Simon mumbled something else I couldn't understand and took off.

"I can't wait for the next meeting, but 'till then, I'll use the nothing as something; I mean I'll use your absence to do some schoolwork. See you tomorrow," I called after him.

10 - I CAN ONLY HAVE SHORT TERM RELATIONSHIPS WITH DRINKS

"Sorry Guys, I need a 'number one' break." Sara glanced at JJ to make sure he'd stop the story until she got back. "You know I can only have short term relationships with drinks. I promise I'll be back in two minutes," she said, and jumped off the couch, heading toward the bathroom.

"Interesting start, Uncle," Gill said. "This boy, Ehud, is a fast learner. I wish I could learn that fast. Maybe if the teachers at school were more like Simon and less like Cinderella's step-mother, I'd be a better student."

"I know what you mean," JJ said. "Both Ehud and Simon are fast learners, and they're both very special to me. They're good friends."

Gill tilted his head a bit to the side. "What do you mean friends? I thought Ehud was you, when you were a kid just like me."

"Ehud can be any kid or adult. You can be Ehud too."

"Yeah, right. I can't get concepts like this. I'm struggling with eighth grade stuff, have you forgotten already?"

"If I were Simon," JJ said, "I'd tell you it's all about your attitude. If you act like an artist, you'll be one. However, don't you worry, the story isn't over yet. Your perspective might change."

"I wish it would," Gill answered, while looking out of the window and watching pigeons landing on the oak tree in the front yard. "By the way, I bet Ehud's mom's character is based on my mom. Homework, homework and homework! That's all she ever talks about. Maybe if she wasn't bugging me so much, I'd have more fun while doing it."

"Maybe if you'd do your homework, she wouldn't have to nag you," David joined the conversation.

"Don't start with this again, Dad," Gill said, immediately defensive. "I do the best I can."

"So how come she always needs to chase you to get you to do your homework?"

"Kids, behave yourselves," JJ said, rising from his seat and sliding the chair back.

"I'm not..." Gill started to speak but changed his mind. He glanced at JJ who slowly sat back down again, his eyes on David.

David sighed, looked at JJ and then at his son. He turned his head toward the kitchen and licked his lips while inhaling the aromas wafting from the cooking food. "JJ, I hope you're finishing your story soon. It looks like Gill is enjoying it, but I'm not sure how long my belly will survive with no food."

"The story is for you too," JJ said.

"I know, but that food is waiting for me," he said, with a smile.

"Dad, why don't you let go of your sense of hunger and maybe learn something new."

"Don't start with me, Gill," David said, looking harshly at the boy.

JJ sighed again and raised his hands and head toward the ceiling as if asking for God's help.

"Did I miss anything?" Sara asked, as she hopped back into the room.

"Nothing important," JJ answered softly.

"Great!" She took her seat and first looked at her husband and then her son. "Do you think that if I surrender, these two will stop attacking me all the time?" she asked, slyly checking to see their reactions.

JJ wanted to burst out with something like: *Enough with the drama! I'm trying to help you guys out here.* He was starting to lose his patience. If you were to put those three in the ring, they would keep fighting until they collapsed from exhaustion. However, he held his tongue and instead asked, "Sis, why don't we just wait 'till the end and see what happens?"

"Okay bro, no need to get all huffy. I just want to make sure I get something out of your story that can help me and the boys."

JJ knew that her sensors detected his lack of patience. *Damn, she's right*, he thought. He needed to listen more carefully to his own story. He took a deep breath and said, "Hey, I'm cool. Should we continue?"

Gill zipped his lips with his hand and turned two curious eyes on JJ.

David tapped a finger by his eyebrow. JJ hoped that even if David didn't agree with everything, the story was still making him think.

Sara relaxed on the couch. Her fingers, which had been digging into her arm at the beginning of the story, were now lightly stroking the irritated skin. She signaled to JJ with a quick nod that he should continue.

He took a deep breath, and surrendered his thoughts and the judgments and reactions that they raised. The smell of the baking roast beef wasn't as spicy anymore.

11 - MAYBE WHAT IS RIGHT FOR ME ISN'T RIGHT FOR YOU

I had quit training at the dojo since the day of my unfortunate Green Belt exam. There were a few reasons for this: first, the test took place just before summer break and I was busy finishing up some big school assignments; second, I was still secretly hoping that Simon would train me, not only in art, but also in something applicable to fighting; and finally, the main reason for quitting was that I felt ashamed to go to the club with my yellow belt, when most of my friends had green ones. I hoped that, as Simon promised, by changing my attitude I'd become a true artist. As a true artist, I'd be able to show my master that he was wrong to fail me. I might even become better than him, or at least better than Tom.

Meanwhile, in order to stay in shape, I had no choice but to train with my cousin, Alon. I hoped that we could have a practice session during his next visit, Saturday morning. We'd practiced together several times in the past, on the grass in the backyard. In Hebrew, Alon means "oak tree." I thought that this was an appropriate name for him. He was a tall, tanned, short haired, ex-navy-seal fighter. I never told anyone, but I was pretty scared of him. He was trained in

Judo and therefore preferred ground wrestling. I, having been trained in Kung Fu, preferred to fight on my feet.

When we got together to practice, the difference between strength and speed was always obvious. Our sessions could easily become a source of amusement for anyone who happened to catch us in the act. During our workouts, Alon looked for close contact so that he could take me down to the ground; I spent my time trying to surprise him by hopping around, up and down, left and right, forward and backward. May usually sat a safe distance away, watching us carefully and moving back when we got too close. Every now and then she'd stretch her neck and let out an empathy howl.

In past practices with Alon, I felt stressed, and my muscles cramped up because I remained cautious and alert at every second. I spent a good portion of the time trying to figure out a way to attack from a safe distance so that I wouldn't get hurt. I usually felt heavy, slow and vulnerable. It wasn't much fun. Unfortunately, I didn't have anyone else to practice with. What could I do? I bet Simon would have an artistic idea on how to remedy the situation.

*****

Simon was seated on our park bench. He wore a funny hat that reminded me of a beret I once saw on an artist who was painting the landscape of the park. I waved at him and waited for a group of cyclists to pass me on the trail.

"How are you, young man?" Simon asked, as I approached him.

"Not bad, enjoying the sunny weather, what about you?"

"Great, thanks. Our last conversation about surrendering did me some good yesterday. I even used it myself."

I gave him a puzzled look as I joined him on the bench. "How?"

"I have been working on a puzzle for a few weeks, and I got really stuck on the part with the grass. It's all so green and looks the same no matter where I try to work on it."

I frowned. "I hate green."

Simon chuckled. "So, I almost gave up. But thanks to talking to you, I remembered to surrender the frustration and I was able to make lots of progress. Half of the grass is done now. Hooray! But enough chitchat, why do you look so worried today?"

"Nothing serious. I'm going to practice Kung Fu with my cousin; I thought you might be able to help. But, before we go there, I have a question about our first meeting."

"Shoot," he said smiling. He had a million types of smiles; and while they all looked different, they always made me feel like everything was alright.

"Kung Fu is an art, not a fight. I think I get that, but besides that, what makes it an art? I think I'm missing a piece of the puzzle about that."

"Excellent question. As I said before, you have more answers than you think. You have your own answers. You don't need to believe something just because it's what I think. Maybe I'm wrong. Maybe what's right for me, isn't right for you. You try to understand my way of thinking but it's difficult. Instead, why don't you try to *feel* the answers inside of yourself? Make the unknown, known. Make the impossible, possible. Close your eyes and visualize yourself as a warrior in the middle of a fight. The enemy is in front of you, attacking you. You're trying to overpower him in the fight. How do you feel?"

I closed my eyes and imagined myself standing in the ring, dressed with my white Kung Fu suit. On the other side of the ring stood Alon, the oak, in his black Judo suit. His eyes glinted at me with a prepare-to-die look.

"Hmmm, I'm totally stressed and kind of scared... Okay, I'm terrified." I said, and opened my eyes to look at Simon and see his reaction. "I felt exactly how I do when I practice with Alon. He's so powerful, he could easily crush someone much bigger than me."

"Very good. Now close your eyes again and this time, imagine yourself as an artist in the middle of a performance. The other player is attacking you and trying to win the game. What do you feel now?" he asked, gently.

I closed my eyes and concentrated on really following his instructions. Artist... Performer... Player... Game... "I feel lighter, like I'm dancing. More flexible. I'm not looking for a fast win, but I'm creating the win. Instead of reacting, I'm acting. I don't feel as small anymore and I'm even enjoying it."

I was surprised by what I was saying. Alon didn't change, he remained the same person. I was the one to change; my point of view had changed. Simon was right. When I tried to *feel* my answers, I understood much better what he was talking about. I was so used to asking for explanations because that's what I'd always done with my parents and teachers. I never considered the possibility that I could find my own answers. When I closed my eyes, if I felt and visualized, I could easily see the difference myself. I was an artist, and an artist could create his own answers.

"Do you still need my explanation?" he asked, while watching a group of people, his age, power-walking around the pond.

I looked at them and wondered if he'd rather join them than spend his time with me and my annoying questions. *Well, he's with me, isn't he?* I answered myself. I turned to Simon and winked. "No, I don't need your explanation. Your visualization technique already did the trick. As a fighter, what I wanted was to avoid getting hurt and at the same time, to hurt the other warrior. Winning was super important; hey, it was everything. There was no fun in it. As an artist, I felt like a dancer. It wasn't a fight anymore. I didn't care who won or lost, there was only the dance. It felt like I was playing. I surrendered and it's kind of funny, but I didn't feel small anymore." It felt powerful to find the answers by myself.

He looked proud of me. "Nice, this is an artist's answer. Anyone can be a warrior. It's easy because we're each trained to be warriors throughout our lives. This is the common approach and therefore accepted as normal. Anyone can struggle, but in wars there are no winners. If two are fighting, both will suffer. Assuming one is stronger, he'll eventually win; but the winner will find it difficult to celebrate the victory because of the suffering he both experienced and caused."

"I think this is right not just in Kung Fu. When I argue with Mom, even if she ends up doing what I want, I never feel like a happy winner."

"That's an interesting point. I can see why you feel this way. The secret isn't in the fight and struggle, but in the art and creation."

"So the artist never fights?" I asked.

"Great question. The artist can fight too. If he's trained well enough he can win almost any battle. But there will always be a better fighter who can beat him. For an artist, the real win is in disarming his opponent without a fight. The greater the artist he is, the less he'll have to fight. However, when he does fight, he does it artistically. Can you imagine how your test could have been different if instead of struggling, you had danced your Kung Fu moves? The act of surrendering would have released your attention from the struggle and the need to win."

"I probably would have enjoyed the whole thing and been more relaxed. I'd probably perform better and improve my chances of winning."

Simon nodded. "Right. Imagine if you could start even earlier with that way of practicing, like at the beginning of your training…"

* * * * *

As I expected, the conversation with Simon helped. I arrived at the practice session with Alon more at ease than usual. Every time I started to panic, I reminded myself that I was an artist and not a fighter.

"Nice practice, Ehud," Alon said, once we had finished up for the day. "A few more like that and I'm not going to be able to keep up with you."

12 - THE ARTIST SEES THE ANGEL TRAPPED IN THE MARBLE, AND CARVES IT TO SET HIM FREE

Two days later, I took May for a run in the park. She wasn't the best running partner, since she often wanted to stop and smell a particular spot or chase after squirrels. However, we tried to be considerate of each other. We had almost finished running a full lap around the pond when I spotted what seemed to be a colorful new statue facing the statue of our city's first mayor. I was curious to see what the new statue represented. I slowed down to a walk and approached it from behind until I was about three steps away.

"If I showed you a marble rock, what would you see?" The statue surprised me with this question. It was Simon, of course. He had been standing completely still, but he finally moved when he sensed May and I were behind him.

"Hmmm... I don't know. I don't know much about rocks. I don't think I ever saw a marble rock. What does it look like? Like a regular rock but just marble?" I wasn't sure where the trick in this question was. "Hmmm... I'd just see a... marble rock, right?"

"Exactly. And if I gave you a hammer and a chisel and asked you to chip away at the marble, what would happen?"

"If I tried really hard, I guess I could break off a few pieces. Where are you going with these questions?" Simon could be very strange at times, but this conversation was more bizarre than ever.

"Try to feel the answer like you did in our previous meeting."

"Okay," I said, and instead of thinking, I visualized the situation. "I struggle with the marble. It fights me, it doesn't want to break. It's weird to feel that; it's no fun. It kind of reminds me of Dad's work. When I was a little boy, he took me to his job once. In those days, he managed a construction site and everyone there worked really hard. They had to cut big wooden boards. And if those big guys found it hard to cut wood, I know how hard it'd be for me to cut into a rock. I'm too weak for that."

"Can you imagine the end result?"

"The end result is an ugly, broken rock. It looks like it got caught in the middle of one of my toy wars from years ago."

He looked amused. "I see that you've had lots of practice in being a warrior. Now, getting back to our exercise, you described what a warrior would do to the rock very well. But you should know that an artist doesn't see any rock. The artist sees something else."

"What do ya mean? How can anyone look at a rock and see something else? A rock is a rock, isn't it?" I asked, and glanced at May, who lay by our feet. She was still breathing heavily after our run. She blinked her eyes and tilted her head. She probably didn't get it either.

"The artist Michelangelo described it as, 'I saw the angel trapped in the marble, and I carved it to set him free.' What he did was similar to what you imagined, but while you visualized struggle, he experienced joy all along the creative process."

"I think I understand what you mean," I said. "If I try to put it into my own words, what you're saying is that the Kung Fu artist releases the victory that is trapped in the battle, right?" I tried to show him that I could follow him without trouble, even though I wasn't sure if I had said something clever or stupid.

"It sounds like a great insight," he responded with one of his famous smiles. "You can choose to treat each situation in life as a fighter or as an artist. Whatever you treat like art, will cause you more pleasure as you do it. It'll make you more creative, earn you more beautiful results, and most importantly, help you reveal your true self, which is the angel under the layers of marble. So, you'll get to know yourself better. Then, you'll be both the sculptor and the statue that is being formed out of the rock at the same time."

"How could I do that? I don't get it."

"Very simple. Your artist is hidden so deep beneath your warrior that you don't even remember your artist is there anymore. When you feel yourself as an artist, you get to know your true self and you begin to discover what you've forgotten. You discover the angel that is trapped deep inside of you. It might seem to you like you're changing, yet you're actually exposing what's hidden. Walking the artist path transforms you from a piece of marble into a marble sculpture."

Two white doves landed on a rock below a tree. I stared at them for a moment and tried to feel what Simon just said, the way he taught me, but I didn't have much luck. "Can you say it again, a different way?" I requested, with hopeful eyes.

"Do you remember how you used to be a stubborn little kid, and then you grew out of it? How did that happen?"

I didn't remember telling him that, yet it was true. "I saw that although my stubbornness helped me to get my way sometimes, it caused me suffering and sometimes made things turn out bad while I was getting there.

"I remember that one day my mom made her famous onion-mushroom quiche. I wanted a piece, but she wouldn't let me have one since it was for the guests, who hadn't shown up yet. I was upset and went to bed, skipping dinner because I was pouting. I wanted to show them both. Mom and Dad went to my room, forgetting the table wasn't ready for the guests yet. They kept asking me to eat a little, but I wouldn't. I was not going to change my mind. In the morning, I woke up and I craved quiche really bad. But it was all gone, and I was the one who had missed out. Because of that I changed. I decided that I'd get my way with my parents without all the drama and the fuss. So, I thought about more creative ways to get what I desire. For example, now I might promise to do something that I usually don't want to do, if they'll give me what I want."

Two soldiers passed us, a man and a woman. Simon waved to them and they smiled in return. "Soldiers are always so young," he said, mostly to himself. He shook his head sadly. "Okay, back to you. You were a fighter. Your wars exhausted you and wore you down. So you decided to surrender to avoid the struggle. Then you learned how to achieve the same results wisely and without fighting. You became an artist. You took one more step forward."

"Yeah, I had become someone different. I changed from being a stubborn kid, to being a smarter one."

"Not exactly," he said. "You didn't change. You were the same. Yet, by walking the artist path and surrendering, you found your way to victory. Your win wasn't at the expense of anyone, so it was like you removed another layer of marble from the rock. Below this layer, you found your ability to get results wisely. You uncovered a latent ability that was just waiting to be discovered."

"So you're saying that this ability was always there, and I just had to uncover it?"

He nodded. "That's exactly what I'm saying."

"Okay, cool. With Mom and Dad I learned how not to fight. But with other things like Kung Fu which, by the way, was supposed to be fun, I struggled and I forgot to enjoy it. I tried hard to break the rock because I wanted to win faster. I wasn't looking to uncover my good abilities underneath all the layers. I didn't try to free the angel. Wow, I was wasting time. What a bummer. If I hadn't acted stupid, I could've already been a Kung Fu artist. I feel kind of dumb!"

"You shouldn't," he said, softly. "So far, you've experienced the struggle. Now you're ready to experience the lack of it. We're all born to be artists, it's just that most of us get caught up in painful ways and we forget we can walk other paths."

"So did you just show up now because I wasn't ready before? Is that what you're saying?"

"Yes. You've finished one stage in your life and now you're ready to move on. I'm here to help you. No step that you take is a waste of time. With everything you do, you peel away one layer after another; just like the sculptor chiseling away at the rock."

"Do you really think that none of my time was wasted? I'm not sure I can agree with you."

"What do you think?" He answered me with a question as usual.

"Until now I was sure it was a waste of time, because if I were an artist a long time ago, I'd be better at everything and I wouldn't have failed the test. But you also said that I have to uncover the artist in me, and that feels right. Until I knew you, I didn't really know he was in there. Sometimes, suddenly I'd feel good and do amazing things that no one, especially I, didn't expect. I get it now. It was my internal artist who did that."

"Right," he said. "To say that you wasted your time is like saying that all the time you spent on your back as a baby was wasted because you didn't crawl. And when you crawled, you wasted your time because you didn't walk, and so on. It's not a waste, it's part of the process. Now you're ready to march forward. It doesn't mean that you weren't as good before and now you're better. You're just walking an endless path. You should do what works for you at the stage that you're in at that time; this way you can move to the next level."

"Thanks. You made me feel much better. If only I was taught that before..."

"I've also lived for years, just like you, in similar situations, with similar regrets and anger."

I raised my eyebrows in surprise. "Really? I thought only I was slow like that."

He laughed heartily as if I'd cracked a good joke. "Not at all. We're much more alike than you think. The time I spent not being an artist is one of the reasons that I am who I am today. It was an important learning process. In any case, it's getting late and I've got to run. Today there is a Bingo game. Alfred must always prevail. He's the most materialistic and competitive person I've ever met. He practically has an electronics warehouse in his room from winning so many prizes. However today, I must win the toaster. I miss the taste of really crispy toast. So in the meantime, your homework is to use the visualization exercise and to *feel* at every opportunity. Practice finding your own answers, so you don't have to rely on those of other people. Just do what you did with me during our last two meetings, and you'll be able to discover your own answers. For every simple question like: Where should I go? What should I do? And who is right? try to feel the various alternatives and imagine the consequences."

I felt great. It felt like I had rediscovered many things that I had known, but just forgotten. I could feel the statue beginning to show up from beneath the stone. I was excited at the thought of the exposed strata and was impatient to find out what other layers I'd reveal. Meanwhile, May had regained her strength; she abruptly pulled me toward a stray tabby cat that passed nearby. I waved goodbye to Simon and gave in to May. She deserved to get her way and move around a bit, especially after patiently lying still for the duration of my meeting with Simon.

13 - EVEN A VETERAN MASTER LIKE ME NEEDS TO BE REMINDED THAT HE'S THE CREATOR OF HIS OWN REALITY

For the next two or three weeks, I didn't thought much about Simon and our meetings in the park. The school year drew to an end quickly. It was time for final exams, goodbyes to friends that I wouldn't see for the whole summer, rehearsals for end-of-year ceremonies and other exciting events. I really liked this time of the year, when school was followed by summer break and a sense of freedom. Also, I needed some time to digest everything that I had learned from Simon. I'd think about him sometimes if I needed to make decisions, if I got angry about something, or if I felt sad. When this happened, I practiced the exercises that he gave me and then, as soon as I felt better, I forgot about him again.

On the last day of school, we received our report cards. My grades were good and met my expectations. I compared grades with the smartest kids in my class and was pleased to find out that I was the best student out of all of the boys. There were only two girls with grades like mine or a little bit better, but they didn't count because they were ultra geeks.

I could imagine the sound of the bell that would signify the start of my summer break, long before it rang. When it finally did ring, I was the first kid to break through the doorway. I burst into the long hallway hopping the Kung Fu dance. I was so into it that I didn't notice Tom, who was passing by my classroom door, and I danced right into him. Really hard.

Tom fell to the floor. I offered him my hand, but he refused it. He jumped back on his feet and looked around, checking to see that no one had seen his humiliating fall. Fortunately, the hallway was still pretty empty, so he didn't totally lose it. I did notice, however, that the color spreading over his face was more vibrant than the red shirt he wore. I also could have sworn that I saw a small tear at the edge of his eye. He rubbed his right elbow and left knee, which apparently were bruised from the fall.

"You're gonna pay for this!" He declared angrily, not meeting my eyes.

"I'm sorry, Tom. I didn't see you. It wasn't intentional." My voice shook a little with worry. I knew he was going to tell his older brother, Rafael, what had just happened. That meant trouble.

"I don't care, you'll hear from my brother!" He shouted, lifting the school bag that had fallen from his shoulder when he hit the ground.

As he turned to leave, I noticed that a green notebook slipped from his bag to the floor. I thought it'd be a nice gesture to pick it up and give it back, but his voice hissed, "You touch it and you're dead!"

I froze.

He picked it up and ran away.

Why was that green notebook such a big deal? I was surprised. What a weirdo. My curiosity about Tom's notebook quickly evaporated, as did the good mood I had been in before my encounter with him. *Why was I such a fool? How could I have made such a mistake? Why wasn't I more careful? Is the same story from last summer repeating itself?* The summer before, Tom had falsely accused me of trying to break his leg in a soccer match; he'd threatened to get revenge. I was so frightened that

I had opted to stay at home watching TV, for practically the entire summer break.

This was the last day of school. I should be happy. Yet, on the way home, I couldn't help but think of the newest terror in store for me this summer because of my recent incident with Tom. I wondered what Simon would do in a situation like this. "Why are there such bad people in the world? Why do they always pick on me?" I asked myself out loud while walking toward my home.

"They're not bad. There's no such thing as bad people. Evil is only one point of view out of infinite perspectives." Simon announced from behind me, making me jump since my nervous system was already strained. For a second, I thought that Tom and his brother might have caught up to me. "I passed by and saw you, so I thought to stop and say hello." He explained, responding to my unasked question as to what he was doing there. But I hardly noticed the question since I was in such turmoil about my summer, about to be spoiled just like last year's.

"Give me a break! With all due respect, that is complete craziness. Of course there are bad people; and two of the worst ones are going to kick my ass real soon!" I blurted out, without even saying hello. "They're nasty kids. They pick on the weak and beat kids up without a reason. They're bad, and you can't view it any other way. I wish they'd both die in a horrible accident!"

A shudder went through his body, like he had received an electric shock. "I can feel your fear of them as if it were mine. Fear creates anger, and anger creates negative thoughts. These thoughts increase difficult feelings, which bring even more awful thoughts and feelings. All of this usually becomes a tsunami of hate. Just like what's happening to you right now. Fear and anger take over and pull you into an inescapable vortex." He wore a fatherly expression as he stroked my head. "Let's try out the visualization exercise that you learned. Imagine Rafael and Tom are approaching, what's going on? What are they doing to you?"

"This is silly. I don't want to."

"Ehud…"

A car honked its horn and made me jump. I forgot to check the road before crossing the street. "Okay. I'll try it just because I don't have a better idea." This time the exercise was more difficult. I was afraid to close my eyes because I felt so vulnerable. I was scared to even imagine them attacking me. "Just please make sure that they don't come."

"No problem. I promise to guard you as if my life depended on it."

I had learned to trust him. I felt connected to him, as if we were one. I didn't know what that meant, but I knew he'd never hurt me. I closed my eyes and imagined that Rafael and Tom had arrived. I could picture Rafael - a big lump of angry muscles - advancing his strides toward me, armed with the look of a murderer. He's taller than both me and Tom, by at least a whole head. Tom is walking fast, almost running, to keep up. He seems very confident and arrogant behind his brother's broad back. They reach me and stand a nose away.

Rafael shouts at me, "How dare you knock my brother down?" Meanwhile Tom, who is partially hidden behind Rafael, curses and makes comments about my mom and sister. Rafael pushes me and punches me in the stomach. It hurts! Tom spits at me from a safe distance and adds a few kicks. Then they both turn and go to find someone else to bother. I opened my eyes. My face was flushed and my lips were pursed. I was bent over and my hands clutched my stomach in an attempt to ease the pain caused by the imaginary fist.

Simon grabbed my shoulders. "Great! I see that you really got into it."

I miserably stared at him in silence, waiting for him to continue.

"Imagine now that you haven't bumped into them yet," he said. "The days go by. You know that meeting them is inevitable. How do you feel?"

I closed my eyes again and began to visualize how it'd be for me, with this fear hanging over my head. Every time I go out, I look nervously around. It feels like a heavy weight rests on my shoulders; it's the burden of tension and a fear of the unknown. I feel agitated.

It's like there's an anticipation of something unpleasant about to happen, it's pressing on my chest. I'd rather stay home and not deal with them. I'm scared that they'll sneak up on me and attack before I have a chance to defend myself.

I opened my eyes. My whole body was shaking, my heart rate was elevated and my face was flushed. That anxious, on-high-alert feeling was so familiar to me. I was afraid of all sorts of things. I had been fearful for so long, it seemed like a black cloud had been following me everywhere. This was an awful sensation. "I felt much worse during the second practice time," I reported.

"I can understand this," he said. "Suffering through cumulative and constant fear is much greater than anything they can actually do to you. This feeling is magnified when you avoid the confrontation with them, because it lasts longer."

My words burst out of me, sounding tense and defensive. "Look, I'm afraid, but everyone is frightened sometimes. Do you expect me not to be afraid at all? Are you such a hero that you never fear anything?"

"I certainly do get scared sometimes," he replied, calmly. "It's natural to be afraid, but it's *not* natural to walk around with fear all of the time."

"But that's how I feel. Am I supposed to be like a robot and control my emotions on a constant basis? Am I supposed to just ignore my fear?"

"If you were to see them right now, standing in front of you, how would you feel?" He returned to his habit of questioning.

"I'd be terrified!" I said, and apprehensively looked left and right. I wanted to make sure that they weren't really coming and that Simon's question was only hypothetical. But apart from a few strangers hurrying by and a mom walking slowly alongside her baby, there was no one around.

"It's natural. Fear is an emotion that appears spontaneously, in response to something that seems like a threat. Now, if you're just walking down the street and you don't see them, how do you feel?"

"If I'm just walking down the street and they're nowhere close by, I don't feel anything special. But if I think about them and the possibility that at any moment they might pop up around the corner, I get very scared."

"That's right. The thought of them causes you to create fear. It's not a spontaneous fear. It's a fear brought on by a conscious thought. So I'm calling this type of fear a thought and not an emotion. When you think negative thoughts like: What if they suddenly appear? these negative thoughts create negative emotions. Can you see that the negative thoughts are causing you more harm than Tom and Rafael are?"

"Maybe," I replied. "Last summer, even though they threatened me, they didn't do much except for calling out an occasional insult. But I walked around in constant fear… or I stayed at home and suffered a lot. I see what you mean. They were the whole reason for my suffering, but I now get how that suffering was also my fault. My fear controlled me, rather than me controlling it. I shouldn't go through another summer in constant fear. I want to overcome this as soon as possible. You said before that I could avoid the confrontation. What do you suggest I do?" I asked, hoping that he had some magic, a miracle, or at least a good idea.

"You have plenty of options. The artist is creative and knows that every problem has many solutions."

"For example?" I said, trying to get a solution out of him, even though I knew that I'd have a better chance of getting water out of a rock.

"Close your eyes, feel and visualize what you could do." He pulled out his famous exercise.

I closed my eyes. "Well, uh… I can send a letter of explanation to Tom; after all, I didn't mean to hurt him," I replied, but I wasn't sure it'd work.

"This is one option, what else?"

"I can also go to their apartment and knock on the door. They wouldn't beat me up in front of their parents. Then I could explain it was all just an accident." I started to gain some confidence.

"This is another good option, what else?"

"Are you sure there are more?"

He grinned.

"Wait, let me try to visualize... Oh, yes, I can also ask Mom to speak to their mom; our mothers have known each other since childhood. Even better, I can ask the coach from the dojo to speak with them; I mean, we have all trained at the same dojo." I got excited. Simon was right. There were infinite possibilities. The more I thought about it, the more I was open to new ideas. It was really stupid to be so afraid. "You know what Simon? I realized that whenever fear takes over, I lose my ability to think logically."

"Me too," he said. "The artist on the other hand creates his own reality and never gets stuck on a problem without finding a solution. We'll talk more about it some other time, now I have to go back to the retirement home. We have a ballroom dancing class today. You-know-who will steal the first dance with Mary if I'm late."

I chuckled. "Yes, I know. By the way, how was the Bingo night? Did you win the toaster or did Alfred beat you, as usual?"

"Funny you should ask. I was very focused on competing with Alfred, but we both ended up losing to Mary."

"Ouch," I said. "So what is an artist supposed to do in a case like that? You said an artist creates his own reality, and here you failed."

He affectionately patted my head. "You are a smart boy. Even a veteran artist like me sometimes needs to be reminded that he's the creator of his own reality. I'm lucky to have you to remind me. I'll feel into it and I'll let you know what I come up with."

Before we said goodbye, we made arrangements to meet the following day so I could teach him to send emails. I was excited. Finally I would get to meet the beautiful Mary and perhaps the scary, evil Alfred as well.

14 - YOU ARE AS GOOD A TEACHER AS I AM

May couldn't join me on the visit to Simon's retirement home. I gave her a goodbye pat on the head and held my hand out to Alisa. Mom had asked me to take her to the park to meet some friends. "Come on Ali, let's go."

We went out into the yard and May followed us through her dog door. Her sad gaze made sure that we knew she was unhappy to be left behind. "We'll be right back, you don't need to worry," Alisa said, while petting May's fur. I pulled on Alisa's hand and we headed out toward the park.

It was the first day of summer break. The sun seemed to be celebrating high up in the center of the sky. The birds tweeted their happy, summer songs. The flowers didn't miss out on the celebration either; they sported their brightest colors and perfumed the air with the smell of freedom. I was armed with a baseball cap, khaki shorts, brown sandals and my fancy blue shirt. Mom had insisted that I wear this shirt, admonishing me, "You don't want to look like a bum."

I left Alisa with her friends by the water fountain at the park's entrance. I waved to the two bored mothers who were watching Alisa's friends, and then I headed toward "our" bench.

"You ready?" Simon asked me when I got there.

"As ready as I can be."

We walked in silence in the direction he usually went at the end of our meetings. We had to go around the pond to reach the far exit of the park. "It'll take us about fifteen minutes to walk there. I can answer your question in the meantime," he said, finally breaking the silence.

I stared at him. "What question? I didn't ask anything."

He winked at me. "You know, the question you want to ask me."

I wasn't sure what he was talking about, so I mentally played back the last conversation from our previous meeting. "Oh, of course." I suddenly remembered. "You said that there are no bad people. I don't agree. You have to explain what you mean."

"I knew it was bothering you. Evil is just a point of view. I'll give you an example. Say you're watching a program where a tiger is chasing a gazelle. The gazelle is running for its life. The tiger is merciless and quickly closing the distance. What's going through your mind?"

"Run Bambi! Run! Don't let the evil tiger catch you!" I yelled, enthusiastically. "I always root for the weaker of the two."

"Now imagine that you're watching television again, this time the program is about an old tiger. Although she's wounded, she tries to take care of her family. Hyenas are trying to steal her starving cubs, but she fights them off with her remaining energy. This old tiger goes on a desperate hunt for food. She needs to regain her strength. She chases after a gazelle that is quickly escaping. It's likely that she and her family will starve. What's going through your head now?"

"Catch him! Hunt him! You must feed the cubs!" I was amazed at my enthusiasm.

"Can you see how your perspective changed? These are the exact same tiger and gazelle; you were just viewing the scene from a different standpoint."

"Wow, I see what you're saying. The same event can look different from different points of view, right? The gazelle was innocent prey in one story but then he was a much-needed source of food in the other one."

He smiled. "That's a nice way to look at it."

"This idea reminds me of a drawing class I took at school. We all sat in a circle around a jug containing five flowers in the center of a table. The flowers came in various colors and sizes. Each drawing was unique because everyone saw the vase and flowers from a different angle." I paused to think. "I can see the distinct perspectives in both of these examples, but I still can't understand how someone who hits me can be good from any point of view."

"From your angle, a bully will always be bad. You're right, you can't see it differently. However he can be seen differently from another angle, like you saw in my tiger example and your drawing example, which by the way, was excellent. Fighting is a ---"

"Ehud, *Kid* hit me!" I could barely understand Alisa. She rushed at us, tears streaming down her face, cutting Simon off mid-sentence. Her face was beet red. Her swollen, wet eyes shot me a humiliated look. Her shoulders were heaving as she sniffled and sucked in gulps of air. I knelt and opened my arms wide. She ran to me and hugged me tightly, her little arms drawing security from her big brother. I knew this boy she called Kid. His real name was Bill, but since he was a bully, everyone called him Bully the Kid. After awhile, it got shortened to just Kid.

"Don't worry, Alisa. After I take care of that little punk, he'll never come anywhere near you again."

"I knew you'd protect me." She wiped her tears and ran off to continue playing with her friends. It was funny how quickly she went from crying to wanting to play.

"I'm sorry Simon, but I can't come with you today. I have some business to take care of," I said, my face burning with anger. "I'm going to bust this kid's face for touching my little sister."

"Take a deep breath, Ehud." He gave me the most reassuring smile so far.

"But this is exactly what I'm talking about. This is the proof that regardless of perspective, some people are just bad. How can a big kid that hit little Alisa, not be bad?"

"If you hit a younger boy, does that make you bad?" He asked, ignoring my little victory.

"I think so. I shouldn't beat others. Whoever does that is bad. I'm sure about that."

"What if the kid you beat is younger than you, but older than Alisa, and he beat her first?"

"It changes the whole picture," I said. "Then I think it's okay. I'm not bad. I'm just defending my sister. He's bad, he hit her. I have the right to defend her." I pounded a fist into my palm. Simon didn't manage to throw me off. "And beat him up is exactly what I intend to do as soon as we finish this conversation." Dark, angry clouds covered the sky obscuring the sun. They seemed to throw a grey blanket over Simon and his logic. Although I kind of suspected that he was preparing a trap for me, blinded by my rage, I rushed in like a mouse after a piece of cheese.

"And if Alisa hit his younger sister first, and he only came to defend her, who's evil now?"

"Oh... Alisa? Alisa is the bad girl? I mean, she's my sister and I love her and she's always a good girl, but if she hit..." I stammered.

"What if Alisa hit someone to protect her friend? Or what if another girl made fun of Alisa in front of her classmates? Or any other story. Can you see how your perspective keeps changing depending on the new information I give you? In reality, you never know the whole story. You don't know what happened first, you don't know what each person was experiencing, what each person thought, or what one person said and how the other reacted," he said, and softly smiled again.

I was a bit embarrassed, but I appreciated that he didn't ridicule me for falling into his trap. If I were him, I'd gloat. Lucky for me, Simon saw the situation from another angle. "So, are you saying that instead of beating Kid, I should first check out what really happened?"

"That would make sense, even though truth is a relative concept and everyone has his own version of it. You should listen to all parties to get a complete picture."

"I guess."

"If you determine that a person is evil, you're choosing to view things from a specific perspective, one that may not be correct from another viewpoint. Even if someone does something that you perceive as evil, he may have a good reason that, from his eyes, justifies his actions. It's just like when you felt that it wasn't wrong to hit if you were doing it to protect Alisa."

I decided that even though this boy, Kid, was super annoying, I'd listen to what he had to say. Despite Simon's logical reasoning, it was still hard for me to agree with him. "What if Tom and Rafael throw stones at a cat? For sure the cat hasn't done anything to them. So are they still not bad? Am I supposed to ignore their actions and do nothing to help the cat?" I asked, a self-satisfied smile spreading across my face.

"Ehud, this isn't an argument. You're right from your perspective, I'm right from mine. I'm just showing you my way, the artist path. You don't have to adopt this way. It's not even one particular path; it's your own road, the one which leads you to feel like an artist. On *my* path, a person doesn't engage in judging good and evil, right or wrong. He accepts everything just as it is. Each judgment imposes a particular perspective and shades the existence of other truths. When I judge something, I'm no longer an artist, but a fighter."

"I can see that." I blushed. "But what did the cat do to them?"

"The cat probably didn't hurt them, but keep in mind that they must have their reasons."

"What reasons could they possibly have to justify hurting a cat?"

"I can't know for sure. Maybe they're unloading frustrations that they collected elsewhere. Maybe someone stronger than them hurt them, and they couldn't get revenge, so they passed on their anger and hurt to a creature that is weaker."

I wasn't sure I agreed with Simon's argument, but it sounded interesting. I didn't know Tom and Rafael well enough to know if that could be true for them.

"Maybe from their eyes, they're just goofing off," Simon added, "and you're the bad boy that bothers them. They don't view themselves as bad kids. You're the one judging their behavior as something bad."

"But everyone I know would agree with me."

"Probably yes, but that doesn't make it necessarily true. And there are other people who may see it differently. You might even change your mind one day. Who knows? We change our values all of the time."

"What do you mean by changing values?" I asked.

"For example, when I was a kid, I fought against ant nests. I filled them with water and covered them with sand. I saw ants as the enemy. Everyone around me saw them like this as well. That was the absolute truth. Today I see it differently and I don't bother them anymore. Ants are looking for food to survive. The fact that I don't like that they invade my kitchen, doesn't make them bad. Think about what you'd do if you were hungry and needed to find food."

"What about wars? Dad says that the enemy is cruel and wants to kill us all. They don't have a real reason to hate us. They're just evil."

"You bring up an excellent question," he said. "I was going to talk about everyday life. People tend to judge everything as either good or bad. I tried to use simple examples to make a point, but your question requires a more in-depth exploration. The question of who is right and who is wrong, rings true even between countries. The perception of good and evil, and the desire to make justice, leads to wars. As long as I think I can win and force my *truth*, why shouldn't I fight what I perceive as evil? After all, I'm the good guy. In war, each side believes that it's good and is fighting evil."

"How can that be?" I asked, perplexed. "In every war movie I've ever seen, there has always been a good side and a bad side."

Simon smiled broadly, satisfied with my question. "The films, like most people in real life, choose one viewpoint. In real war, there are two good sides, fighting two evil sides. This is the paradox of all wars. It's even more complicated; sometimes, within one side there are people who oppose the war. They believe the war is unnecessary. They choose a different perspective. They might then be considered 'traitors.' Some people may say they aren't good, even though they're on the same side."

"So are *they* the real good ones?" For a moment I was confused.

"From one standpoint, yes..."

"And from another, no," I completed his sentence.

"Exactly, I'm glad you understand. Sometimes, the enemy of yesterday becomes tomorrow's ally. Every time you think about someone or something as bad or good, you choose one perspective. In my way, this isn't possible."

"So why do most people do that?"

"I guess they like the drama. Who likes to read a book with no villains?"

"You're funny," I said.

Suddenly a cat jumped out of a garbage can perched on the curb. I realized that Simon had made me forget all about Kid and we had started to walk again. I watched the cat arching its back; it made a nasty, hissing sound at another cat, in an effort to claim whatever food had been discovered in the trash.

The cats reminded me of a question I had. "I can see how it's easier to label someone as your enemy than it is to check his viewpoint. But what about the cat that Rafael and Tom threw stones at? Do I let them kill it? I think letting them kill a cat seems like an act of evil."

"You're absolutely right, from your viewpoint. The philosopher Edmund Burke said, 'All that is necessary for the triumph of evil is that good men do nothing.' It's natural to want to help the helpless. Do your best to save the cat, don't hesitate. When someone attacks you, defend yourself. Don't let anyone hurt you. Don't be a victim, but if you attack someone who abused a cat yesterday, trying to revenge his evil act, you're just like him. Now you're bad from his eyes; he didn't do anything to you, yet you attacked him."

"So where is the boundary? Where is the line between saving, defending and attacking?"

"What do you think?" He, of course, answered my question with another question.

"I don't know. I doubt there is a clear boundary. Hey wait a second, boundaries are also a point of view, aren't they?"

"This is an excellent answer. Each one of us draws his own boundary lines. In your world, you'll have to determine your own standards. In my world, when I feel that it's time to go to war, I check what's motivating me. Is it love or anger? If I save a cat, it's because I love animals. If I'm defending myself, it's because I love myself. But if I want to beat someone who abused a cat yesterday, I know anger took control."

I kicked a small stone with my sandals as I walked. "So, I'm supposed to let them get away with it?"

"There are better ways to make someone stop abusing an animal than to attack them. I'm sure that if you think about it, you can find some. Try the exercise we did yesterday; feel and visualize the answer."

I liked hearing his explanation. He challenged me and made me strive to seek my own answers. He also didn't expect me to adopt his point of view. "It goes against everything I have learned. I've always been taught that there's good and bad, and that I should be a good boy."

"I know. This is the conventional approach in the world. The good knight who fights the evil dragon. Like you said before, thousands of movies have been made on this subject. In movies, like in reality, power is justice. Whoever has the power forces his perspective on those who are weaker; and thus that viewpoint becomes right. The most powerful force gets to decide what's right and what's wrong. That's why, for most people, victory is the most important position possible. It's fine that there are losers, as long as you're not one of them. Anyone who differs from you can easily become the bad guy or the enemy. That's just my opinion. You can adopt it or you can choose to stick to the conventional approach. The choice is yours."

"It's hard for me to accept what you say, even though it sounds right. I need some time to think about it."

"That's certainly understandable. Your entire life you were trained to divide everything into the categories of good and bad. I was too. When I started to view things from different angles, I found out that everything is right from a particular standpoint. It takes great courage to recognize that there are other perspectives while examining your own beliefs. However, it's well worth it."

"Are you saying that the line that divides two people who argue is the perspective they have chosen?" I checked to make certain that I understood correctly.

"I didn't say that, but it's true. The points of view that we adopt are what distinguish us from one another. We all want the same things in life: happiness, success, love, peace, health, satisfaction, self-expression, respect and so on. What differentiates us is that we each have varying ideas on what's the most effective way to achieve these things. Therefore, each one of us chooses the viewpoint that seems most appropriate to him, or the one he has been told is best suited to this purpose. That's why we handle matters in such different ways. Take your time. We can discuss good and evil in greater detail again soon."

We arrived at the retirement home which looked more like a resort. The first thing I saw was a woman of about sixty-five, with well-styled hair and a cute, turned-up nose, wearing an elegant cream-colored sundress. She seemed quite content sitting outside in the garden under a flowered umbrella which stood between two palm trees. An older man sat next to her. He was about the same age as Simon. His hair was graying but his back was surprisingly straight. They both rose to meet us.

"Mary and Alfred?" I asked Simon, even though I knew the answer.

"Indeed you're right," he confirmed. "Hello, dear princess," he said, and kissed Mary's outstretched hand. "Hello, Alfred," he said to his bitter enemy, in a bloodcurdling voice.

"Hello, Simon," Alfred said, in a voice even more chilling. Those two could make it feel like winter on a hot summer day. They glared at each other for about a minute while they slowly circled around Mary. I waited with tense anticipation for their next move.

"Why are you standing there like a dummy?" Alfred flashed a smile first. "Give me a hug. The child will think that people our age have nothing better to do than have stupid fights."

Simon approached Alfred to give him a hug. "But you're the one who starts all the fights."

Alfred winked at me, entwined in the hug. "I don't fight with you, I just show you your mistakes."

"Every day, the same epic adventure," Mary said, smiling at me. "Those two, it's an endless love story."

"You're from the U.N., remember? You're not supposed to intervene." Simon stuck out his tongue at her. They all laughed heartily and invited me to join them for a cool glass of lemonade. Before we went off to the computer room, Simon whispered to Mary, "Once I become an expert in sending emails, could we stop by for some crispy toast?"

"Of course, it'd be my pleasure," she replied.

We said goodbye to his friends and headed on our way. "Yesterday you helped me to return to the artist path. I created my own reality again." He tapped on my shoulder and smiled mischievously. "Thanks to the artist path, I realized that there is a great advantage in the fact that the toaster is in Mary's room. Now I have a perfect excuse to stop by."

"I'm glad to help," I replied. "Now I have another question. You explained that there's no right or wrong. It's all just a point of view. So how come you call Alfred evil?"

I saw him blush for the first time. "You're absolutely right. You're as good a teacher as I am. I need to be reminded of the path often, don't I?"

ONE-LEGGED SEAGULL

* * * * *

I showed Simon how to send an email and how to open attachments. Together we sent a message to his son. Then I asked him to try sending an email to his grandson. He started a new email, wrote a subject and typed his message, but then got stuck. "Oh, I don't think I'll ever be able to do this myself."

I chuckled and looked up at him quizzically. "Did we forget to be artists again?"

He stroked his brow. "Yes, I know. I guess it's your job to remind me over and over again. It's the path I know by heart, but I continue to wander off of it. I know I'm close. I forgot only the last step." He quickly returned to himself.

"Right. If you want to send the email to your grandson, choose his email address, click 'Send' and you're done." We continued to practice for a few more minutes. At the end of our tutorial, as promised, he was an email wizard.

15 - YOU CAN'T TEACH AN OLD DOG NEW TRICKS

JJ stopped his story to take a sip of cold water from his metal bottle.

"The student is already instructing the teacher," Gill said. "What's going on?"

JJ slid the bottle back onto the coffee table. "Wait and see. The answer to all of your questions will come later in the story,"

Gill rose from his chair. "It takes too much patience."

"What's new? Just like when I ask you to do your homework," Sara said.

"Do you see how she makes me nervous?" Gill said, while sitting back down.

JJ joined both palms to his chest as if begging. "Please don't start again."

Gill softened. "Okay Uncle, just for you. But before you go on, I have a question. According to your story, people shouldn't punish, right? So if I don't punish someone who did something bad, how would he know that he was wrong?"

JJ took note that for the first time that day, Sara really smiled. It was a half-smile, but still a real one. The three listeners looked at JJ expectantly, waiting to hear his response. "Do exactly what Simon taught. Practice the exercise to find your own answer."

Gill seemed surprised. "An evasive answer, but I like it. You want me to walk the artist path like Ehud. I'll do the exercise after the meal. Meanwhile, please continue, I'm dying to hear what the story of this Simon dude is. I feel like he's got a secret that he hasn't revealed yet."

Sara seemed pleased with JJ's answer. "I usually know what I want, but sometimes I just can't seem to be able to make choices. I think I can use this exercise when I'm confused. Maybe it will help me to be less uncertain when it's time to make decisions."

David on the other hand, still seemed unconvinced. JJ could feel his resistance to some of the ideas introduced in the story. "David, don't look so worried. It's just a story, you know."

David scratched the back of his head. "Yeah, just a story," he muttered. "Do you mean that anyone can be Ehud? Anyone can be an artist? I mean, I can see how it might help Gill, but frankly, as much as I might need it, I can't see it working in my world."

"Why not Dad?" Gill jumped in before JJ had a chance to reply. "All you have to do is practice what Simon taught."

"I don't know." David's voice was melancholy. "I think I'm getting too old for that nonsense. My father used to say that you can't teach an old dog new tricks."

Sara leaned her head sympathetically on David's shoulder while looking at her brother.

Gill wore a deceptively serious expression. "Who knows, maybe your dad was wrong. And besides, you're not that old in dog years. You're only six." His comment drew smiles from the group. "Well Uncle JJ, are you going to continue or are you waiting for us to get so old that we can't learn new tricks?"

"God forbid. Here I go."

16 - THE BIG CONFRONTATION

I had always been fascinated that the best and worst days started out no differently than every other day. This particular mid-summer morning began like any other, with a mission to get some milk for Mom's coffee. I walked to the neighborhood grocery store whistling a happy tune. I had forgotten all about the R.A.T.s - the nickname I gave Rafael and Tom, the neighborhood's scariest villains. Following Simon's advice, I did my best not to obsess about how painful a meeting with them could turn out to be. He was right, because not thinking these negative thoughts had saved me from all the bad emotions they could have caused. My summer had been great so far.

I entered the store and waved to the hunchbacked clerk.

"How are you doing today, son?" he asked, while tapping absently on the huge cash register which was probably as old as he was.

"I'm good, sir, thanks. What about you?"

"Not too bad myself." He tipped his head with a little smile. "How is that little sister of yours doing? I haven't seen her lately."

I inhaled deeply to enjoy the smell of the fresh bread wafting from the shelves to his right. "Alisa is almost as busy as I am. Last week I had to play the big brother role a few times, accompanying her to some play dates. She'd rather go on her own, but Mom insisted that I go with her."

"You're a good kid."

While he went on to discuss the bratty neighborhood kids and many other unimportant topics, I waited for just one short sentence. "That'll be eight-seventy," he finally said. Hearing the price and knowing it meant that I could escape from the store, satisfied me almost as much as the candy I added to Mom's list. I paid him and took the bag he offered. I liked the guy, but man, could he talk a person into the grave!

I bounded out of the shop with the bag tucked under my arm. Oh, Shit! I swallowed back a scream. What are the odds? Just when I was thinking of a grave, I spotted the RATs. They were standing a block away, by a red-roofed duplex, picking on a small, freckled boy. The few people in the street seemed to all be minding their own business. None of them seemed to care enough to rescue either that kid, or me. Even though the RATs hadn't seen me yet, fear froze my body.

A few seconds later, though I was still unnoticed, my legs began to shake like the pictures in a homemade video. My mind raced, trying to come up with a good escape plan. I found none. How about becoming invisible? It'd be a great solution, if only I could. How about running away? This wasn't an option. Rafael, a dazzling athlete and the school's running champ, was much faster than me. If he saw me trying to run away, it'd only provoke him.

I glanced at them again to make sure I was still off their radar. Even though their backs were toward me, it felt like their shadows were already on top of me. I imagined them sneaking between the SUVs on the street, hiding behind poplar trees and planning their lynching strategy. I could almost hear them whistling the creepy tune that played in my favorite horror movie whenever someone was about to die. What should I do? Simon! Yes, Simon! "I need you here now!" Feeling quite hopeless, I whispered a prayer.

As if by magic, a big hand wrapped itself around mine. My heart leapt. It was Simon! I was so thrilled to see him, that I didn't even consider how he had again mysteriously appeared out of nowhere just when I needed him. I was saved! I was about to scream with joy, but then a disturbing thought crushed my elation. *Could an old man like Simon really help me against those two bullies?* Nope. They are going to kick both our asses.

"Simon?" I sent him the kind of look May gives me when she knows she is in trouble, but hopes to get off scot-free. I clutched the paper bag from the shop in one hand, my fingers clenching and unclenching around it, while Simon held onto my other.

"Remember what we discussed the last time we met," he whispered.

It had been a long discussion, but I had a strong feeling I knew what he was talking about. "We all want happiness, success, love, serenity, respect and health. The difference lies in our idea of how to achieve these things. This is what makes us all seem so different; that's what makes some people seem good, others bad, what makes some seem right and others wrong. That's what you want me to remember now, right?"

"Exactly!" he confirmed. "Keep in mind that Rafael and Tom are kids, just like you. Not only do you share similar goals, but you have all three experienced suffering, disappointment, grief, sorrow and failure on your life's journeys. We're all taking this journey; and sometimes while we're trying to avoid being the prey, we unintentionally become the predator."

I knew what he was trying to do. The moment I started repeating these ideas in my head, and really *feel* it, the brothers changed shape. They were no longer as chilling as before. Rafael wasn't as big as I had always perceived him. They were both just kids, like me. It reminded me of a line I once heard, something like, "If you prick them, do they not bleed? If you tickle them, do they not laugh? If it's raining, do they not get wet?" For the first time, I didn't see the RATs as enemies.

Then, just when I started to feel better, a car passed us and the driver almost hit a careless pedestrian. The scream of the wheels made Tom turn around. He saw me and tugged on Rafael's sleeve, pointed at me and whispered something in Rafael's ear. Rafael looked in my direction and motioned for me to wait. He crossed the street between two parked cars and strode toward me and Simon quickly, ready to rumble.

"It's show time," I said. I watched Rafael, and my eyes wavered between perceiving him as a kid, like me, and a mad engine, racing at full throttle to crash into me.

"Who you talking to, Owly?" The nickname I hated so much sounded less like poison this time. I turned to look at Simon, but he was already gone. Unfortunately, it seemed that magic could work both ways. I felt my stomach tighten and realized I couldn't get any words out. I encouraged Rafael to continue speaking with my eyes.

"I heard you have a new hobby these days, beating up smaller kids," he barked at me from a few inches away.

I stopped breathing and just stared at him. Thanks to my conversations with Simon, I could now see that from Rafael's perspective, I might be the bad guy in this story. I *had* been the one to knock Tom down on the last day of school. It was an accident, but they might see it differently. Maybe Rafael is just playing the role of big brother, protecting his younger sibling exactly like I've done many times for Alisa. What a weird world! Each person has his own viewpoint and therefore views any situation differently from those around him. But we many times assume that our perspective is the only one, and that therefore everyone shares it.

Rafael cut into the thread of my thoughts, "So is this your new thing, jackass?" he asked, pulling on my shirt collar, the rage in his eyes piercing through me.

I ran through Simon's ideas over and over, it was like Mom searching every possible location for her lost glasses. My mind went blank. *I should say something quickly,* I thought. I looked at the RATs. Rafael stood there overly confident in a ridiculous purple flowered shirt, and wild upright hair. Tom wore an elegant green, and probably fake, Lacoste shirt; his dirty blond hair was combed and slicked back neatly. He half-hid behind his brother's back. Since I was less terrified than usual when faced with a confrontation, I was experiencing both of the boys differently. To my surprise, I noticed that Tom exuded insecurity, and it kind of reminded me of myself.

Still wordless, I examined Rafael's eyes. I saw anger floating in an ocean of pain. *Where did all of this pain come from?* I asked myself. Then, without warning, my mouth started talking. "Your brother has a steel head." I couldn't believe that I dared to answer Rafael, the frightening Kung Fu fighter, in this way. But even more surprising than that, I had spoken to him while looking him straight in the eye, as an equal.

"What are you talking about, dude?" he asked, puzzled. There was no doubt that I had surprised him. I could see his eyes slightly shifting. I had captured his interest so that some of his anger was taken over by curiosity.

"On the last day of school, I was the first kid to leave my classroom," I began. "I boogied the freedom dance out of the room to welcome the start of the summer break. I didn't expect anyone else to be in the hall, so I rushed out without actually looking around. That's when I accidentally bumped my arm into your brother's head. It still hurts a bit." I rubbed my left elbow with my right palm for effect. Rafael listened and I gained confidence. "I think that Tom was so shocked by the fact that he hurt me, that he took off before I even had a chance to apologize for running into him. Now, when I saw you guys coming over, I thought it'd be a good time to say how sorry I was for being so careless. I also thought Tom might be glad to know that my elbow doesn't hurt as much anymore... even though his head is really hard." I finished, hoping that the bully had a sense of humor. If not, I'd be in big trouble.

While waiting for Rafael's response, a deafening silence fell over the neighborhood. It drove out the sound of car horns, tweeting birds, and the conversations of people around us. For the moment, it was just Rafael, Tom, and me in a bubble that was on the verge of explosion. They examined me for a long while, and the silence seemed to last longer than the time it takes to drive through midtown Tel Aviv during rush hour.

I glanced at Rafael, looking for any sign of what he was thinking, but his face remained expressionless. Years ago, I had heard my dad calling it, "a poker face." When I asked Dad why it was called a "poker face," he grinned at me and offered the most annoying answer of all, "You'll understand when you grow up." Now I feared there was a chance that my growing up was never going to happen.

After a few more seconds, which seemed more like months, Rafael changed his facial expression. His face softened, muscle by muscle. His eyes lit up and his lips formed a smile, pushing away the angry leftovers. "You are funny, Owly chump. Next time, I hope you look where you're going. Another guy might not have as good a sense of humor as I do. You were lucky this time, but you don't want to test someone else," he said, with a slightly paternal tone to his voice.

Tom, still behind his brother's wide back, seemed confused. On the one hand he seemed amused by the conversation, but on the other hand he wasn't getting to see the conflict he had probably hoped for. Eventually, humor won out over disappointment and Tom chuckled as well. Rafael landed a friendly slap on my chest. My whole body shook. I couldn't stop myself from imagining how a less friendly meeting with a guy like him might have ended. No one would want to upset this mound of muscles.

"Be less clumsy, Owly. Don't forget - not every dude is nice like me." He repeated his friendly warning in a deep and pleasant voice. He turned to Tom and said, "Chop-chop bro, we're done here. He's funny, this Owly boy. I don't think he'll ever mess with you again. He's too afraid of you, Mr. Brick-Head."

Tom didn't look amused at all by the new nickname he had "earned." He obligingly dragged himself behind his brother like a shadow. A few steps later he stopped for a second and turned his head toward me. We fixed our eyes on each other. His look was different; what I had always perceived as demon eyes appeared now to be just regular kid ones.

* * * * *

I couldn't believe my luck. If it wasn't for Simon showing up at the last minute to rescue me, the RATs would have eaten me alive. I looked around and identified Simon seated on a shaded bench across the street. I felt like jumping on him and smothering him with hugs, but I was too embarrassed to do that with strangers all around. Instead I said, "Thanks, man. The magic you pulled really saved my backside!"

"I didn't do anything. You did it all. The compassion you felt when you realized that they were kids just like you, helped you to see them as people, not enemies. You used humor to break the tension; you were able to transform their anger into amusement in an artistic way." He seemed to be almost as happy as me. "Compassion is so powerful that it not only changed your attitude, it changed Rafael's as well. You were a real artist today, I'm so proud of you."

"Did I do all of that?" I blushed. "Still, I couldn't have done it without you."

"You deserve all of the credit," he insisted. "You avoided a fight, thanks to walking the artist path. I could only introduce you to this path, but it was your choice to walk it. Not everyone is brave enough to abandon the warrior's way. It's not easy to change old habits after being a warrior for more than twelve years."

I slumped down on the bench next to him. "Yup. Today I could see the difference between the two paths. As a warrior I'd have gotten defensive with Rafael and maybe even tried to blame Tom. Neither of them would've appreciated that. The alternative, artistic approach worked like a charm. Tell me more about the artist path."

Simon's eyes twinkled. "The artist walks the journey with awareness. He's aware of the feelings of others and respects those feelings. His honesty and integrity make him recognize that he's responsible for his own choices and the outcome of those choices. He's wise, tolerant of what is different, and he looks for peaceful resolutions to conflicts. He doesn't take anything for granted, appreciates all of the gifts that the world offers him, and constantly asks himself questions. In fact, a good artist must make sure to have more questions than answers. It's these questions that encourage him to stay on the path and keep learning and experimenting. He's never right or wrong. He steers his way skillfully along the river of life, yet never drifts."

"Sounds like the way I want to live. How can I be an artist too?"

Simon flashed one of his widest smiles and said, "Being an artist is exactly what we practice in our meetings, kid."

Surprised, I had to think about that for a second. "Okay, but I don't have the patience to wait and learn the slow way. Are there any shortcuts? Can't I become an artist faster?"

"Not that I'm aware of." He grinned. "I spent years looking for shortcuts, and I only found frustration. You become an artist when you think and feel like one naturally and without effort. Until then you have to practice the path."

"How?"

"Practice what we have learned. For example, practice feeling more compassion for others. Challenge yourself everyday to see just how compassionate you can be, exactly like what you did today. It'll help you to avoid the feeling of separation between yourself and others."

"What do you mean by feeling of separation?" I asked.

"Every time you identify a difference between yourself and someone else, you subconsciously pull yourself away, and separate yourself from them. You automatically tell yourself, 'This is like me and this isn't like me; this is good and this is bad; this is more *something* than I am, and this is less *something* than I am'. The story of separation is always the same, it's just the *something* that changes."

I scratched my head. "So you are saying it's bad to compare? But we get graded at school. The temptation to compare is too high. I want to be the best."

Simon chuckled. "I know what you mean. Sometimes it's difficult. I want you to think of a basketball team. Each one of the players has a different position on the court, they have different qualities and heights. They can't compare themselves, they need to play as a team. What would happen if one of them said: 'I'm the tallest, and therefore I should have the ball all the time'? No one player can win a championship without the help of his teammates."

"You mean that we all have different roles in life and therefore have different qualities, right?"

Simon gave me a thumbs-up and a wink, the same gesture I use with my friends when they know the answer for a hard question. "I love the way you put it. By comparing, you notice, create, and then expand your experience of separation. When you feel separate from anything - a person, an idea, a feeling or a situation, you become indifferent to whatever you have separated yourself from. If you make this a habit, then eventually you don't care about anyone that isn't like you; this is one of the reasons that there is so much hatred in the world.

"People start to adopt the idea that if something isn't similar to their way of being, thinking, living or believing, it's wrong or bad and so it doesn't matter. When you feel separate from another person, you're losing your connection to them as a fellow human being. When this happens, you squash your ability to imagine what it's like to be in their shoes or experience their suffering, so you don't feel care or compassion for them."

I squinted up at him, curious. "So should I pity them?"

"Pity isn't compassion. It's a way of feeling superior. Pity says, 'I'm better than poor, weak and unfortunate you.' These feelings don't benefit anyone."

"I think I can see that," I said. "And I'm familiar with separation. It's how I felt about Rafael and Tom until today. They were different. They were bad."

"Right. Unity, on the other hand, creates harmony. Compassion has the ability to disarm the negative energy that forms obstacles. That's how you triumphed today. You were able to diffuse a frightening situation without fighting and without designating any roles of winner and loser. You overcame negative energy and you conquered fear. You defeated anger and you prevented both yourself and your enemy from suffering. Great job! This is the artist path, the compassion path."

"It's the same thing I found before my last practice with Alon. The artist works *with* people instead of competing and struggling against them. This is why the artist never loses and never becomes a victim, right?"

"Very well said. Your wording of this idea is inspiring," he said. He almost looked surprised at my unexpected wisdom, but it was clear he was pleased, too.

My head felt clear. I was thrilled. It was as if I had just won a new belt. This was the most impressive victory I could ever remember, and the best part was that there were no losers. Everyone was a winner. After that day, neither Rafael nor Tom ever bothered me again. None of us would've guessed it then, but a few years later we all became good friends. Many things had become clear to me after that encounter, yet I was still too young to understand my father's saying, "just because you win a battle, doesn't mean you win the whole war."

17 - ONLY IN MOVIES DOES THE HERO WIN THE BATTLE AGAINST EVIL AND RIDE OFF INTO THE SUNSET

"Nice story, Uncle, I like it. But you need to explain how this guy Simon appears whenever Ehud needs him." Gill rose from his seat once again to stand behind his parents.

"Already walking away? The story isn't over yet. I promised you that all of your questions will be answered by the end," JJ said, and nodded his head to signal that Gill should return to his chair.

"What do you mean not over?" Gill marveled. "Ehud had the big confrontation. He won. Shabbat Shalom, thank you and good luck. End of story."

David looked at JJ, puzzled. "You're kidding us, right? I thought the story was done and we could all go to eat now."

Sara pulled a tissue out of her bag. She wiped a tear from the corner of her eye. "It was an exciting story, so what now?"

JJ smiled warmly, he was happy that his story touched her. "Only in movies does the hero win the battle against evil and ride off into the sunset. In reality, this victory is just the beginning of the rest of the journey. A hero must continue to persevere on his path. Each day should be treated as the first day of the rest of his life. Ehud still needs to discover how to stick with the artist path, learn more lessons, overcome even higher obstacles, take the Green Belt test again, uncover Simon's secret, and find out how and why his path intersected with Simon's. Do you want to miss all of that?"

Gill shook a vigorous "no" with his head and returned to his chair. In contrast, David rose from the couch and stretched his limbs. "JJ, if the meal is delayed today, thanks to your long story, at least allow me a little break. I need a cup of Turkish coffee. Anyone else want a drink?" JJ and Gill shook their heads and David walked out of the room. Sara took advantage of the break to visit the bathroom again.

"Uncle, I have a question that might sound stupid," Gill whispered, looking in the direction of the hallway. "I understand that you're trying to help, and the story's great, but how exactly does it relate to my problem?"

"That's a great question. What's the problem you are trying to solve?"

"You mean other than my inconsiderate parents?" Gill glanced again at the door. "I always fail tests. This is probably because it's hard for me to sit in one place to study. Also, I always procrastinate studying until the last moment and then I never have enough time to prepare. It's just too much effort. The whole thing is hard for me to deal with, and I can't seem to fix it on my own."

"Ehud has a problem with tests too."

"Yes, but it's different with him. He has Kung Fu problems and friends issues. I mean, he's kind of a nerd. I have no problems like that at all."

"Are you sure?"

"A million percent. I'm one of the coolest boys in class." As if on cue, his cell phone beeped indicating an incoming text message. "You see how popular I am?" Gill grinned and paused to look at the screen to see who had sent the text. His face fell.

I guess Gill had been hoping for a message from someone other than the sender, JJ thought. "Okay," JJ said, trying to bring Gill's attention back to their conversation. "So I invite you to figure out which of the tools Ehud has learned about, can be used to solve your problems. I'll check in with you again when we're done. Deal?"

"Whatever you say, Uncle. I trust you."

Sara returned to the room. "What are you guys whispering about in here? What did I miss?"

Gill smiled mischievously at JJ. "Mom, why don't you surrender the feeling that you're always missing something?"

Sara narrowed her eyes. "You're so smart, huh? JJ, when are you getting to the part of the story where Ehud learns to respect his parents? I think Gill can use that lesson. I never talked like this to our folks."

"Why do you pounce on me? I was just kidding," Gill said.

Sara's expression seemed to tighten up, and the light faded out of her eyes. "Watch out, son."

"Who exactly do I need the watch out for? A coward like you? You're afraid of everything, even water."

Sara's face turned red, she opened her mouth to say something, but nothing came out. She coughed until she found her voice. "JJ, do you see what a cheeky child I raised? I don't know what to do about him anymore."

"Come on guys, calm down, I am continuing with the story," JJ said, ignoring their back and forth attacks and signaling to David, who had returned holding a cup of hot coffee, to sit on the couch. *I need to practice more compassion*, JJ reminded himself. *It will help me keep cool with this family, which seems to enjoy fighting all of the time.* So he repeated to himself: *Sara, Gill, David and I all want happiness, love, and serenity. We've all experienced disappointment, sorrow and failure on our journey. We're all students in the school of life...*

"Wait," Gill piped in. "I'm sorry Mom. I didn't mean to say that. If I could take it back, I would. I'm just annoyed about something else. It has nothing to do with you." He glanced at his cell phone. "I apologize for taking it out on you."

Sara looked surprised, in spite of herself. "It's okay, Gill, just try to be less... teenager," she said.

JJ hid a smile. He could feel a wave of peace washing over the room.

18 - IN ORDER TO BE A GREAT ARTIST, YOU MUST BE WILLING TO BE AN AWFUL ARTIST FIRST

In the days following my confrontation with the RATs, I was on top of the world. I felt like an invincible artist. Even though I was on cloud nine, somehow I still felt grounded as well. My back felt straighter. I smiled at the world and it responded with its most beautiful smiles. Nothing that happened upset me or made me feel like any less of an artist.

One hot afternoon, Dad came home from work early and promised he'd take me for a bike ride once the weather cooled down a bit. I was excited; a bike ride with Dad was a rare event. When I felt this excited, I needed to do something to release some energy. Unfortunately, it felt like someone had lit up large ovens in the sky. Anyone who dared to go outside baked in the heat like a piece of steak on the grill. I had no intention of being broiled in the yard. Because of the sweltering heat, my friends were confined to their homes as well, presumably sticking close to their ACs.

While waiting, I started to kick my soccer ball around the living room. Mom and Dad have never given me a brother, and Alisa preferred to play with dolls or watch TV, so I had no choice but to play with and against myself. I played *forward* and took a shot at the imaginary goal; then I quickly ran to the other side to play *goalie* and save the goal. My imaginary tens of thousands of spectators cheered and encouraged me, "Ehud! Ehud! Ehud! ..." I was the best forward and, at the same time, the best goalie.

May happily joined the game; she'd never miss out on any activity involving a ball. I liked how she playfully growled at me while using her front legs and mouth to try to steal the ball, with admirable doggie skill. She nipped at me, catching my pants here, my shirt there, and immediately releasing her grip, careful so as not to tear any clothing. I was glad for an active partner. I had to concentrate in order to keep the ball from her. All of my attention was focused on her and the ball. May also seemed to be in deep and joyful concentration. She wagged her tail continuously while rushing back and forth, trying to get the ball.

Whoever said that the higher you climb, the more it hurts when you fall, was absolutely right.

"May, nooooo ..." I shouted, but it was too late. She was too close to the short table in the center of the living room. Her tail, wagging excitedly, hit the vase. The vase flew to the floor making a wide arc. It was almost as if it enjoyed the unexpected flight; yet, only when landed on the floor and crashed noisily into a million little pieces did it realize the magnitude of this disaster. Fragments of the vase lay scattered all around the room. May was frightened by the noise and fled into the yard through her door.

A broken vase is bad. I stiffened and couldn't move. No really, I literally couldn't move because I was barefoot and the floor was covered with too many shards of glass. Dad and Mom were sure to hear the ruckus from their room; they were probably already on their way to investigate. I knew they wouldn't be happy.

Dad arrived in the living room first. He was shirtless and his white hair was wild. He froze for a second, his eyes almost popping out of his head, his mouth open and his palms on his cheeks. "How many times have I told you not to play ball in the house!" he demanded loudly.

If I remembered correctly, he had told me at least a million times. But obviously this request was too difficult for me to follow, or I'd have obeyed him. After all, I was usually a good boy. I didn't dare to answer him. Meanwhile, Mom joined us. She was wearing a yellow bathrobe and pink slippers. She stood by the living room door, her narrow hazel eyes shooting me looks of blame. She glared at me as if I had broken the vase on purpose, just to shorten her life.

I wanted to cry but, of course, I couldn't. Dad continued to yell at me and I felt like a soggy sponge. I tried to explain that neither I, nor the ball, was responsible for the broken vase. It was May who hadn't been careful. But no one listened. A poisonous, black cloud of victimization began to strangle me, climbing from my stomach through to my lungs, and then up toward my throat. I had to get out of there.

After what seemed like hour's worth of shouting, Dad turned his back for a second to look at Mom. Maybe he got tired of screaming and wanted her to take over for a bit. I jumped on the opportunity and fled out of the room on my toes, trying not to step on the broken glass. However, at that point, getting a cut took a back seat to taking any more rage from my parents. I stormed into the yard, slamming the door behind me in a gesture that informed Dad, Mom and the rest of the world that I'd have no interaction, of any kind, with anyone until further notice.

I hate! Hate! Him! Them! Myself! I thought that I was on the road to becoming an artist, but apparently I had just had beginner's luck with Tom and Rafael. I wasn't really artist material. "I'm a failure!" I quietly screamed to myself, while hiding between the fence and a large bush, so mom and dad couldn't see me.

"And you really believe that?" Simon's whisper came from the other end of the courtyard. I turned to him with a look that combined misery, anger and surprise. He knelt down on the grass and stroked May who sat next to him, shivering with fear, in the space between our house and Dad's shed. I hadn't noticed the two of them until now. She cowered, terrified by the crash of the fallen vase and the shouting that followed.

I tightened my mouth; if I had been able to cry, now would've been the time to do it. I had been so concerned with myself that I hadn't even considered May or how distressed she must have felt. I had disappointed everyone again; not just May, but Simon too. "I'm never gonna be an artist," I moaned angrily as I joined them quickly, making sure I stayed invisible from the windows or door of the house.

"In order to be a great artist, you must be willing to be an awful artist first. Failure is the key to success, that's how you learn." Simon spoke to me soothingly and finished, as usual, with a question. "Have you ever watched a baby learn to walk?"

I swallowed with a long gulp. Silently, I looked at him sitting crossed-legged on the grass in front of me. He was smiling calmly, like a peaceful island in the middle of my ocean of inner misery. It made me feel a bit better and I managed a faint reply. "Yes. Alisa learned to walk a few years ago. It was pretty funny. At first she'd take one step, fall and then sit on her bloated diaper, looking around, as if she didn't understand how she got to the floor. A few seconds later she'd take her next step. After walking a little bit further every day without falling, she eventually walked."

"That's right; a baby falls thousands of times until he learns to walk. It's natural. The secret is in practice and perseverance. He needs to fall in order to learn how to walk. Imagine if Alisa gave up and decided after the first, second, or millionth fall, that she'd never be able to walk because she just kept falling."

I quietly chuckled. "She'd still be crawling,"

He nodded in agreement. "Failures are natural. Every baby knows that so he keeps trying, even after a million failed attempts. Babies are natural artists. When an artist wishes to master a new art, he knows that he must begin as a rookie. He allows himself to fail until, with infinite practice, he becomes a great artist."

"Are you sure? That's how it works?"

He winked at me. "Don't believe me. Try it and see what happens."

"So then I'll be a perfect artist? And nothing bad, like what happened today, will ever happen to me again?"

"Incidents like this might still happen to you sometimes."

I was disappointed. "Really? Why?"

"Look at your life as if it was a conversation; like you are communicating with someone invisible. Life---"

"How can I talk to someone invisible? Can I hear Life?"

"Not exactly. Life talks to you with your experiences, and you answer with your choices on what to do next."

"How exactly?"

"When something happens to you, the repercussions of your previous choices are a kind of a message Life sends you."

"Is that true with anything that happens?"

"I believe so. It can be even as little as a thought you have, like, 'I'm so lonely'."

"What do I do with this message?"

"Make a new choice whether to perceive it as an artist or a warrior. This choice is your answer to the message. The new result of your choice is a new message. Many times you can't move on to a new choice without accepting the previous result. Life is a collection of experiences. The way you experience something is determined by your choices. Results are just check points for you to see what choices caused which results. It's the endless conversation we call experiencing life."

"So I'll never be a perfect artist, right?"

"The goal is not to be perfect, but to do the best you can at every moment. Then you'll never be sorry that you didn't do enough, because you've always done the best you could. Also, your odds of success in any given moment will be higher."

I gestured May to come closer to me and hugged her. She licked my face, and it seemed like she had totally forgotten about what had just happened. *She is so lucky to be able to do that,* I thought. "It makes sense to do the best I can," I said.

"It makes sense, yet there are things that will continue to hold you back from doing so. Here's an example, only a few days ago you were an artist, and now you've convinced yourself that you can't be one. Are you doing the best you can at this moment?"

"I'm trying, the vase wasn't my fault. Who puts a vase on a short table like that anyway? It's so difficult to always be an artist; it's easier to be a warrior and just blame someone else. I just don't---"

"Ehud, are you doing your best?"

"Damn. I guess not," I replied. As hard as it was for me to accept it, he had raised an interesting point: It was me who didn't believe in my ability to be an artist anymore. This belief hurt my chances of being one. "But why did this happen to me? What's the source of my lack of faith? I feel like some strong, outside force made me lose my faith."

Distracted by banging sounds, we looked into the street at a crew working at the edge of the road. Two workers started to drill into the pavement, making a lot of noise. Simon waited a long moment until they stopped, and another worker went back to digging a hole near the curb.

"In order to help you understand, I'll introduce you to two twin brothers, Perfecto and Doubty, who live in your head. Both of them constantly drill into your brain like these two guys in the street. They try to sabotage your thoughts, and that in turn, can often control your actions. Perfecto says things like, 'You're too young. You're too old. Be sensible. You're not good enough. What are they going to think about you?' and so on. For him, everything has to be perfect or it's a waste of time and you shouldn't even try. He un-inspires you. If you weren't born an artist, he'll make sure that you never become one, since being a rookie is not an option. He's creative in his attempts to sabotage your success."

I was familiar with these ideas. They had dampened my efforts to achieve what I wanted plenty of times in the last twelve years. Yes, it seemed that the infamous Perfecto had just now convinced me that I could never be an artist.

Simon continued with his explanation. "Who is your worst enemy?"

If he had asked me before the confrontation, I'd have probably said Tom. Fortunately, we had resolved our issues; a few days before we had even greeted one another when we met on the street. "What do you mean my worst enemy?"

"Who always blocks you from getting what you want?"

"Um, I'm not sure... there's always someone or something that interferes ..." I stammered.

"Right. You always have an excuse, 'It's too hard for me. I'm not a lucky person. Someone interrupted me. I didn't understand...' Doubty is your biggest enemy. Just like his twin brother Perfecto, he also poisons your mind convincing you that you have no chance of succeeding. He's to blame for the lack of faith in your abilities. He makes you feel less sure you can succeed by generating doubt. If you don't listen to him, you'll always be more successful."

"You described exactly how I feel now," I said. "I don't feel like I can ever be an artist, it's so frustrating. So how do I get rid of these mind bullies?"

"It's simple. Instead of searching for who to blame, talk to both Doubty, your inner doubt, and to Perfecto, the perfection enforcer. Tell them, 'Enough! I don't need you! Go away!' They'll get offended, at least temporarily, and leave."

I smiled a sad little smile. He knew how to make me feel better, even when I was in a crisis and life looked like an endless walk down a dark alley. "Why do they even exist? What's their role? Why do things like the broken vase incident happen to me? Why can't I live a problem-free life?" I felt like I was pouring today's lava from my volcanic eruption all over Simon.

"I guess you like the challenges, otherwise you might be bored."

"Bored? Well, I suppose I might be, but what can I do instead of living like this?"

"You could view every event as an opportunity to assess who you are and, based on that assessment, create who you want to be. The vase broke, your Dad yelled at you, you were offended. Now the question is how you are going to use those occurrences?"

"What do ya mean *use*? How can I *use* something like that?"

"Remember how you told me that May is a master at surrendering? How she makes the best of what is presented to her? The vase incident happened. You can't go back in time and prevent it. Will you continue to choose frustration and anger, or do you want to choose to be an artist again?"

"But how can I? I can't control all of that."

"Even if you can't control events that happen, you can always choose your response to them. Your response is the only choice that no one can ever take from you."

I felt my despair lift a bit, pushed aside by the warm wind of hope that his words inspired. "So how can I be an artist again?"

"Can you recall what you did the last time you felt this challenged? What is the artist path?"

I took a deep breath and let out a sigh. "Let's see... I think I can start with compassion. Right? It helped like magic or even a miracle last time." I began hesitantly, trying to draw encouragement from my memory of the encounter with Rafael and Tom and our conflict-free resolution. "This time, I was offended by my dad. Fathers should be supportive, tolerant and loving; not jump up screaming at me when I make a mistake. It was just a vase. That's why I got offended." I continued hesitantly, explaining to both myself and Simon how I strayed from the artist path.

Simon seemed pleased with the direction our conversation had taken. "Your idea to start with compassion is simple, yet brilliant; it's the idea of a true artist. But even more amazing is that in thinking about compassion, you uncovered an idea that you hold, a belief inside of you that when your father fell short of your expectations, it naturally caused you to feel offended. Does your belief that fathers should be supportive, tolerant, loving, and not come into the room screaming, help you in this case? Or is holding to that belief hurting you?"

I looked at Simon, baffled and defensive. "I don't think it's a belief, it's a fact. Fathers should be relaxed! Um…but I do see how believing that way has prevented me from being compassionate toward my own dad."

"Fact is not reality, it's just a belief that you hold with absolute certainty; but let's forget the terms. How is it affecting you?"

"I'm not sure I agree, but now that I found this fact or belief about my dad, I can see things somehow differently. Now, my dad seems more like a person, who sometimes gets angry just like I do."

Simon looked at me quizzically. "So what do you want to do about it?"

"He's my dad. He's a grownup, but he used to be a kid just like me." Without really noticing it, I began to feel compassion again. "Even today, somewhere deep inside, he's still a kid. He loves to play, tell jokes and make funny faces. He has dreams and wishes. He has experienced success and failure, just like me. I can see how upset he was by the fact that I was playing ball in the house and broke the vase. In all fairness, he *has* forbidden me to play ball in the house." Suddenly I saw my father in a different light. "I don't really hate him. I love him and want him to love me back. I want him to prove to me that he loves me no matter what. I'm angry when he doesn't show it, like when he shouts at me. I guess, in this case, the belief that he should show his love all the time hurts me," I concluded.

"Amazing work , Ehud! You simultaneously examined your beliefs and experienced compassion."

"Thank you, I feel better now. The compassion thing seems to work every time I do it."

"I'm glad you see how easy it is to return to the artist path," he said.

"With you on my side, yes. I feel like I created a new reality, a different, more pleasant one."

"You did. The easiest way to change the world is to change the way you look at it. Today you discovered that you can create your reality by choosing a point of view. Feeling compassion changed your perspective. This is only one of the ways to create a desired reality."

"What are other ways?" I wanted him to continue and teach me more. Oddly, straying from the artist path and then returning to it gave me more confidence. Knowing I could find my way back again made me feel more sure-footed than just learning about it and experiencing the single success with Rafael and Tom. I was determined to learn any trick that could help me avoid repeating the same mistake I had made just an hour before.

Simon inhaled and then exhaled very deeply. He stroked his bald head gently, as if considering whether to stop the meeting here or to continue with the lesson, at the request of his persistent student. He frowned. "You sure you have the patience to continue with long explanations? If I stay, I'll miss my ice night with the gang."

"What's ice night? Which gang?"

"At the retirement home, we have a group that we call The Young Gang. Most members of the gang are younger than seventy-five, although being young is less about actual years and more a matter of approach. Samuel, for example, a celebrated eighty-five-year-old, joins us for practically every meeting; yet Joel, an 'old' man, a bit older than sixty, has never joined us. Every Thursday, our gang goes out for ice cream at the mall; we call it 'ice night.' Today is Alfred's turn to pay. If I stay here, I'll miss the pleasure of eating ice cream with Mary, on Alfred's dollar." He looked at me, checking my reaction to what he had just told me.

I made May-eyes at him. May has taught me that May-eyes can be a powerful manipulative tool to be used when one wants something but isn't getting it. Simon kept me in suspense for a few seconds before deciding. "I had a great time with you, Ehud, and I'd give up on ice night, but I think you have discovered enough insights for one day. We should leave the rest for another time."

I didn't like his decision, but he was probably right. An artist doesn't rush, but finds his own natural pace. "Is there a chance that I can join the gang?" I asked.

"Gladly. You're young like us, in spirit that is. Mary and Alfred keep asking about you, and the others want to meet the little genius who taught me how to send emails. I'm certain that they'd love to have you join." He made me blush.

I put on a pair of my sandals that were lying around in the yard. I hugged May good-bye and promised that I'd be back soon. Then I joined Simon, who was waiting for me on the sidewalk, and we headed towards the mall. While we were walking, I used my nail to mark an "x" on my arm, so that I'd remember to remind Simon to finish his list of suggestions on how I could create my desired reality.

19 - WHY IS IT SO HARD TO SAY I'M SORRY?

The gang was really happy to see me and I enjoyed seeing them too. Simon was right; being young is really a matter of feeling young. After spending time with them, I realized that the Young Gang was more like a group of naughty kids than a group of elderly folks. They played tricks on each other and the conversations they had were hysterical. Knock-knock jokes were a favorite, but they also told some adult jokes that I was probably not supposed to hear. On the way back from the mall, I decided to ask Simon about something that had been bothering me. "May I ask you two questions?"

"Sure."

"First, how did you make it to my yard, just when I needed you? I never even told you where I live. I was so upset at the moment when you appeared, that I didn't even pay attention to the fact that you actually showed up again just when I needed you."

"Let's just say that I sensed you'd get into trouble and you'd need my help. So I let you magnetize me. I came to your neighborhood and walked around, and then suddenly I saw an agitated May jumping through a doggie door and hiding. So I decided to sit with her and wait for you to join us. What was the second thing you wanted to know?"

His story sounded too perfect, but I was very eager to hear more ways to create my own reality. I decided not to press the issue about him appearing out of nowhere, as if by magic. "I think I'm ready to continue learning your list." He looked at me, puzzled. "You know, the list of ways that I can create my own reality. Can we do that now?"

After a brief pause, he decided to go on. My determination to learn and his will to teach trumped the concept that we had gone over too much for one day. "Let's start with the examples you already learned and take it from there. If you give Doubty, your inner doubt, control, you'll never do new things because you'll be convinced that you're going to fail. Even if you do try, you won't be determined enough, on account of the doubt. And that will lower your chances of success. If you feel doubtful, you'll never do your best. You'll just 'try' instead of 'doing it'. Doubty steals your greatest creative power. He takes your faith. The most important ingredient in creating your desired reality is genuinely believing in your own abilities."

"And then there's his brother," I said.

"That's right. You'd better learn to ignore Perfecto, as well. Perfecto keeps you from using three of the tools most important to the creative process – learning, training and practice. Without them, no one can become an artist. Even the most talented musician must practice for hours every week in order to be a great performer."

"Perfecto and Doubty sound so much alike."

"Right. It's because they are twins." He smiled fondly at me. "They both have the same impact, but they attack you from different directions. While Doubty makes you question your ability to succeed, Perfecto belittles your wins so he can convince you to quit."

"What a pair of crooks. What else?"

"You also saw that the very events that divert you from the artist path, can also lead you further along, set you deeper onto the artist track, and strengthen you. Life is a process rather than a struggle. It's the process of realizing what you are, defining what you choose to be, growing into that person, and continuing that approach over and over in a loop. One particular incident could be a traumatic disaster that you'll never forget, or a wonderful gift that contributes to your growth."

"I saw this today," I said. "Do you have any tips on how to make sure my experiences will turn out to be a gift, and not a traumatic disaster?"

"You have to reprogram yourself with awareness and practice."

"What do ya mean?"

"Sometimes you're programmed to automatically feel bad about certain events. If someone calls you names for example, it's an insult, and the "rule" says you should be hurt. Realizing that is awareness. You don't have to get hurt. You can practice choosing how to feel, deliberately."

"It's not easy."

"At first choosing what to feel takes effort it's true, but then, after practice, feeling good will become a habit. Experience is not what happens to you, it's how you choose to feel when things happen to you."

"Gotcha. Anything else?"

"Your belief system is like a dirty glass, and you see and create the whole world through it."

"Huh?"

"When you believe that the world is a bad place, you see it, through this thought, as bad. It's not really important if it's bad or not. You'll see it as bad, anyway. When you think that something is impossible, you're not able to make it happen. When you choose to be angry, you see the world through anger; and when you love, you see the world through love. Which thoughts do you want to choose? If you choose to be an artist with just one thought, you'll earn a day on the artist track. If you practice the artist path every day, it will become your path."

"I didn't know that beliefs have so much power," I said.

"Yeah, they're so strong that, even if something is right under your nose, you won't be able to see it."

"How is it possible?"

"If you believe that Rafael is a nasty, disgusting bully, that's how you're going to see him. You'll miss the goodness in his heart, you won't see his pain, or that he's just doing the natural thing by protecting his brother."

"Ha, yes, I discovered that in our confrontation. What else?"

"Always make the right choices."

I raised a skeptical eyebrow. "Great advice, very useful."

"Why the sarcasm?"

I squinted at Simon, perplexed. "What's sarcasm?"

"You said one thing, but you meant something else."

"But how am I supposed to know what the right choices are?"

"Simply by learning."

"What kind of learning?"

"The learning that happens whenever you make bad choices," he said, and winked at me.

I chuckled. "Alright, so you mean I should dare to practice and overcome the fear of making mistakes. This way I'll be able to learn from any mistakes I make. I already know that."

"It's more than that. Making any choice is mostly better than not making one, even if you end up making a bad choice. Choices keep you moving, otherwise you're stuck. In the long run, the everyday choices that you make can all take you to the same place. Instead of meticulously calculating your next step, just choose your next adventure and then go with it."

"I see. By the way, what exactly makes a bad choice? You said that everything is relative. So, there's no good or bad."

"Great question," he said, and closed his eyes, probably visualizing the answer. "A bad choice," he continued after a few seconds, "is a choice that doesn't serve you. It stops you and keeps you away from your goals; it won't bring you long term joy. A bad choice is made in the reaction mode; it ignores the lesson to be learned from the experience." He also seemed to be learning as we went along.

"How do I know I'm in a reaction mode?"

"Blaming someone else for doing or not doing something is the best sign that you are reacting."

"Got it. What else?"

"You can use the visualizing exercise here as well."

"How exactly?"

"First sit quietly and clear your head from any thoughts. Just be. Hold the experience: *I am*, and let go of everything else. Feel the power of nature and the endlessness of the universe. You're one drop in this ocean of life. Feel what it's like to be part of this ocean. You're connected to it. You're the ocean. Nothing is impossible for this ocean, even if it takes some time and several attempts. Close your eyes and really imagine how *having* what you want, feels to you. Feel that you deserve to have it. Then don't just imagine having it, but feel that you already have it."

"And that's it? I'll get what I want?"

"That's not all. Of course you need to take action. You also need to identify the beliefs that discourage you as you go along, and then recognize that they're just beliefs. They're nothing more than obstacles that can be overcome. Uncover which emotions, like fear or frustration, stop you. Then deliberately surrender them, like we learned."

"With the visualization exercise, right?"

"Right. Once you reach the point where you feel like you have what you want, trust the outcome of the exercise and surrender the need to pursue this desire. Do you know why?"

I tried to clap my hands on an annoying fly that had been buzzing around us. I missed it once, and then again. I followed it with my eyes while walking and almost stepped into a lamppost. "Ehud?" Simon asked.

"Huh? What was the question?"

"Do you know why you should surrender the need to pursue your desire?"

"Yeah, I think so. Because the path is more important than the goal. Right?"

"You got that right."

"Cool. Next." I smiled.

He chuckled. "You want it all, don't you?"

"Of course."

"Choose the right goals for you."

"How?"

"What are you passionate about? What would make you proud? What do you enjoy doing? What can you do that will help others? Answer those questions and you'll know your goals."

"I get the first three questions, but how is helping others relevant?"

"There's a great satisfaction in helping others. If you never tried it, you should; then you'll see. Just do it."

"You mean like when I make Ali happy it makes me happy? I guess that actually… whenever I make someone else happy, it makes me happy. I think I got it. Look at this. They agree with you."

Simon turned his head in the direction I pointed, toward two huge billboards. One was an Adidas ad which read, "Impossible is Nothing," and the other was a Nike ad which read, "Just do it."

Simon smiled. "Yeah, if you just do it, impossible is nothing."

"Sorry that I went off on a tangent there. So, hmmm, it seems like there is a never-ending list of things to practice."

"The truth is that until you asked for a list, I never gave it thought. Your questions made me think, so the list grew. There are a million other ways, but since you're already an artist, you can find them yourself."

"I know, but please give me just one more tip before you leave today. Okay?"

He looked me over. I could see that he was thinking. "Alright. Just one more, then you'll have to complete the list yourself." He took a deep breath. "There are only two emotions that determine which point of view a person will pick. Want to guess what they are?"

"Hmmm, anger and… love?"

Simon chuckled. "Close, you got one of the two. Not bad."

"Really? Which one did I miss?"

"It's love and fear."

"Fear?" I asked.

"Fear is really the lack of love. People can risk their own life, without fear, to save a loved one. This is possible because where there's love, fear cannot exist. It's almost like flicking on a light switch. If you turn on the light, the dark disappears. If you're afraid, you've wandered away from the path of love. Then suffering will appear, as a reminder to get back on the love track."

I shook my head. "I'm not sure I agree. Sometimes you love so much that you're afraid of losing your loved ones. I love Alisa, but I fear that something bad might happen to her because she's so innocent and fragile."

"When you love, you just love. Fear of losing love or who you love is fear, not love. You can alternate between fear and love all the time, like a light switch going on and off. But once you love, there's no fear. Fear appears only when you forget to love. Anytime you veer from your path, identify the source of your fear."

"Why can't I just experience love?"

"Fear, like a shadow, is created when something blocks the love, or in this example, the light. Even in the most brightly lit room, there are still shadows. Your mission is to love your shadows. Whenever you fail, then you meet the fear."

"Okay, I can see that, but how come you say that there are only two emotions? What about other emotions, like anger?"

"Anger, jealousy and frustration are just fear in disguise. You're mad because you're afraid that---"

"That I'm not loved. That's why I get mad at Mom and Dad sometimes." I completed the sentence for him.

"When you're jealous..." he said, and let me finish.

"I'm afraid that someone else got what I deserve."

"Nice. And when you're frustrated?"

"I'm worried that I can't do something. I understand. Other feelings arise out of the two basic feelings, love and fear."

"That's right. Try to examine which of your beliefs pushed you off the path. Which beliefs, however true they may seem, are preventing you from turning on the light? Figure out what scares you. What are you afraid of losing? What do you think is going to hurt you? Feel compassion for yourself and the world around you. Then you'll see that you're on the artist path."

I thought about what he said. I create my reality in a million different ways. "You're basically saying that I can use any and every incident that occurs, in my favor, to create a better reality. If I choose to create the reality I want, I'll enjoy the outcome. That's what happened in the confrontation with Rafael and Tom, when I chose compassion. If I don't make a choice at all, I'm also creating a reality, but then I'm not directing it. That's when the consequences can be unpleasant. Right?"

"This is a great way to look at it. Again you're showing me something I already knew, but in a different light."

"Thanks. I think I really get it now. So, in every moment, in everything that happens and in every choice I make, I'm actually choosing between the way of love - the artist path, and the way of fear - the warrior path. I never knew that I had the ability to create my own outcome."

"I consider that insight to be one of the most important secrets of life." He nodded and stopped walking. He turned his head to the right, looking at something.

"What?" I asked.

"Yesterday I turned down this road by mistake instead of taking the next right."

"And?"

"I found the prettiest dead-end street, with a great little café that serves the yummiest apple pie." He smiled.

I chuckled. "That's a real artist's attitude, turning a wrong turn into an adventure. You know Simon, I thought about it, and I can see that forgiveness is also an important part of the artist path. I'm gonna forgive my father for shouting. I'll also forgive myself for not listening to him and for not being more careful while playing with

May. Wow, I feel better already. Anger just made me feel miserable; all it did was get me off the path."

He seemed happier than ever. "You see, you're already racing along just like an artist. Forgiveness removes the internal poison that anger creates. You should use it more often."

"I can see that, but people don't always deserve my forgiveness."

"It doesn't matter. Forgiveness is important for *you*. It helps to avoid the pain and suffering you experience every time you think about the offense. Forgiveness is healing to *your* soul."

"Alright, but how do I know when I've truly forgiven?"

"You know it when you no longer respond to the event or person that offended you. Then the hurt stops."

"If forgiveness is so good, then why is it so hard to apologize?" I wondered aloud. "Once, I had a fight with Dad and he didn't talk to me for a whole week, just because I didn't apologize. I didn't tell him that I was sorry because I wasn't. I knew I was right and he was wrong. Eventually Mom showed me that, in the end, I was the one who lost. Regardless of who was actually right and wrong. I couldn't win because my stubbornness and righteousness stood in the way. Mom also said that even if I couldn't see it, Dad felt hurt by our fight too. So at last I told him I was sorry and he immediately forgave me. It was so simple but, at the same time, so hard."

"It's difficult to forgive because all your life you learned not to forgive. You practiced standing your ground no matter what. Many people mistakenly consider forgiveness to be a prize that they're giving to the undeserving person, the offender who caused them pain. Instead, forgiveness should be viewed as a gift to the forgiver."

"So how do I forgive? How can I make forgiveness easier?"

"You already know."

"Hmmm…compassion?"

"Two gold stars! Compassion creates an opportunity to forgive, it frees you from the pain. If you find it difficult to forgive, you can picture forgiveness like a test that you need to get a high grade on, and look at the recipient of your forgiveness like an instructor who came to prepare you for the test. Forgive anyone who has ever hurt you, forgive yourself for every mistake you ever made, forgive destiny for every disaster it's dropped on you. You'll feel much better. You'll have to practice a lot of compassion, since there are so many ways to feel bad about things that happen. Consider it a homework assignment."

"Thanks. So with the exercises we learned today, I can create anything I want?" I asked, and started to fantasize about all the things I want to create.

"This is a great question. Most people I know are using these tools to try and create physical things, but most of the time we actually want to create a certain feeling. We want to feel love and we try to achieve what we believe will make us feel it. But really we can simply create the feeling of loving ourselves. This works with any feeling, all you have to do is think and believe; for example, 'I'm happy', or 'I love myself', or 'I have no worries.' If you do this, soon enough, your feelings will transform. This ability can save you time, energy and frustration."

"It sounds amazing, but how do I create a feeling?"

"Think of a time that you felt happy."

"Alright."

"Try to feel that way again. Don't use words, just feel."

I sat down on a nearby bench beneath a shady tree, and Simon dropped down beside me. I closed my eyes, and spent three minutes on the exercise. "Wow, it feels good. I didn't know it'd be so easy."

"It is easy."

"I think I heard Dad talking about this once. He called it positive thinking."

"Not exactly. It's deeper than positive thinking, it's positive feeling. When you think positively, you temporarily replace a negative feeling with a positive thought. But this doesn't work for long, since the old feeling is still there, creating new negative thoughts. Positive thoughts can't release or transform negative feelings. On the other hand, when you create positive feeling, good thoughts will flow naturally and easily because feelings create thoughts."

"I see. So, are you saying that I can use this exercise to feel good no matter what is going on around me?"

"You bet." He grinned.

I raised an eyebrow. "So how come people don't create the feeling of joy but instead get stuck with suffering?"

"I think many people prefer to stay unhappy and in their comfort zone, rather than have to change their habits. Or, they just don't know how to do any different. Keep in mind that you have to be willing to invest some effort in order to achieve real happiness. Other people aren't aware of this possibility and some just forget they can actually get to where they want to be. But there's a purpose for suffering. Suffering reminds you that you forgot to feel love and joy."

"The next time I suffer, I'll remind myself." I said, then paused. "Okay, but how can someone be happy when there are many bad things happening in his life or around him?"

"Fair question. Let me teach you an exercise that I learned from a Rabbi many years ago. It starts with a list. You spend one hour, not less, creating a list of all the things you're grateful for in life. Like your abilities to see, hear and feel. Your family, your health, your friends, May, your wisdom, and everything else you have in your life that not everybody else in the world has."

"What do you mean? Everybody can see, everybody has family," I said.

"What about the blind? Or the orphans?"

"Ha, okay, I see. Can it also be something like breathing? A month ago I caught a cold. When I finally got better, I was grateful for being able to breathe through my nose and sleep through an entire night."

"Absolutely! This is a great item for the list. When we take everything for granted, we forget to appreciate the gifts we have."

"Yeah. Like walking. It doesn't seem like such a big deal, but when I broke my leg I missed being able to run whenever I wanted to."

"Okay, so you know how to create the list. Once you're done, prioritize your list. Which items on your list are the most valuable to you?"

"What do you mean? You want me to choose between being able to walk, breathe, or see? That's impossible. And how can I choose between my dad and my mom? My list is going to have lots of things which are totally valuable."

He winked. "I think you already got the idea of the exercise. I think you know how anyone can make themselves feel happy, right?"

I laughed. "Nice trick, Simon. I think I understand how this exercise can create a sense of happiness, and I'll do it, so I can experience it firsthand. But you know, something is still bothering me. If I'm content and satisfied with what I have, I might lose my drive to achieve more."

He stretched his arms out wide. "You're really thinking today. Well, here's what I think. First of all, happy people are known to be much more energetic and ambitious than depressed people. And also, if you can't be grateful for something as important as eyesight, how could you really be grateful for, say, a gadget that you'll get bored with in a few weeks? If you take everything for granted, nothing in life will ever give you joy. Nothing!"

"Gotcha."

This was a very exciting day. I fell, but then chose to get up. I transformed a bad day into a happy and beautiful one. I turned a disaster into a valuable lesson. Once again I'm an artist, and I choose to practice and continue walking the artist path. I choose to release the fear of falling. *Why should I be afraid of falling if I can get up again?*

20 - I NEED TO FIND SOMEONE LIKE HIM AS WELL

"Uncle, I protest," Gill interrupted the story.

JJ looked at him curiously and asked, "What's wrong?"

"This Simon dude is a... some kind of a weird magician? I need to find someone like him as well. Then I'd get fat A's on every test. He could help me, like he helps Ehud. And no one could say I'm cheating because he'd appear and disappear at will."

"Maybe you already have someone like him but you're just not aware of it."

"What do you mean?"

JJ winked. "Patience, my dear nephew. Remember what I promised?"

Gill shook his head impatiently. "That all my questions would be answered by the end of the story?"

JJ smiled halfheartedly as he surveyed his audience. Then in a voice which pretended to be insulted he asked, "Is that all you understood so far from the story? That you need to find someone like Simon?"

Gill glanced at his mother. "Not at all. I actually think I'm beginning to understand how I can use this story in my life."

JJ looked at her too. A few minutes before, out of the corner of his eye, he had noticed Sara watching her two men. As she discretely examined them, her expression softened. Maybe the story had encouraged her to practice feeling compassionate toward them. She stroked Gill's head as he sat beside her, and put her other arm around David's shoulders.

"What?" she asked, suddenly noticing JJ's eyes on her.

"Nothing, just checking that you're comfortable."

"Everything is fine. I think I've already learned some tools that can help me achieve more peace. I'm interested to hear more. You can continue."

"Yes, go on," Gill said. "I too want to hear what else I have to learn."

"No problem," JJ said, while he studied David who was looking thoughtful. He knew that David was a fighter and, true to the way of the warrior, every new way scared him, though he would never show it.

David looked at JJ. "Hmmm, I don't know. It's just sounds too good to be true."

"I know. I feel that too sometimes," JJ said. "The thing is, it works."

"Uncle JJ, are you going to continue *today*?" Gill asked.

"Yeah, sure. Just a lil' patience, buddy."

21 - YESTERDAY'S ENEMIES

"Ehud! Ehud!" Kid shouted loudly from the street, with no regard for the neighbors who were taking an afternoon rest. I rushed out of the living room and jumped onto the porch searching between the colorful rose bushes to find Kid.

"What's up?" I demanded of Kid, who leaned against a stop sign.

"Hurry up, there is a fight!"

I burst into a run after him. In the past, I'd have been excited to participate in a fight. Now I was going only because curiosity tugged at me. A group of fifteen excited kids, mostly members of the Kung Fu club, had gathered in a building's almost empty parking lot across the street from the soccer field. They were standing around Rafael and Tom when Kid and I joined them.

"... this is our right and no one's gonna take it from us!" Rafael was animatedly finishing a speech.

"The kids from the other neighborhood took over the soccer field. They're not letting us play." Kid updated me with the details. Since I had spoken with him about "attacking" Alisa, or should I say separating her from another girl, we had became friends. His description of the event differed from Alisa's account. In his version, which proved more reliable, the two girls decided to investigate how firmly each other's hair was rooted to their heads, and Kid had just tried to separate them. I was glad that I hadn't followed my original plan, but instead opted to talk to him before beating him up.

I looked around and found myself amidst a herd of small fighters who were now running toward the soccer field through an avenue of poplar trees. The kids from the other neighborhood were already waiting for us on the field, ready to battle. I'd attended this kind of "meeting" before and knew it'd result in a few bleeding kids, a million scratches, some broken teeth and bones, and many angry parents. I could feel the tension in the air heralding the coming danger and bloodshed. Rafael stood in front of our group, shooting threatening looks at the other gang. It was led by BJ, their version of Rafael. His gaze was no less menacing. His real name was Joseph. BJ was just short for Big Joe, and wow, was he big and ugly!

I was amazed that Kid, Rafael and Tom, who I had considered enemies until recently, were now my allies. *Can it always be so easy to switch from opposing to supporting each other?*

BJ raised a long wooden 2x4 above his head. He must have "borrowed" it from a nearby construction site. "Let's get this over with once and for all," he shouted. His heated gang of followers agreed, cheering and waving chains, sticks and knives. We showed our own enthusiasm for the approaching battle, responding with fighting roars like those produced during Kung Fu training. Abby, also known as Abbruce Lee because of his Bruce Lee hair style, stood slightly behind and to the left of Rafael. He threateningly began to demonstrate his Nunchaku skills.

I have to stop this fight, I thought. I walked out from the middle of my group and stood next to Abby. "Wait a second!" I heard myself shouting. To my surprise, they all stopped what they were doing. Everyone waited to hear what the "four eyes" nerd had to say. The truth is I had no idea what to do next.

"Simon? Where are ya? I need you now! It's time to magically appear," I whispered. I closed my eyes waiting for the magic to happen again. I felt something brush by my hand. I eagerly opened my eyes and was disappointed to find that what I felt was just a butterfly landing on my wrist. I looked around, but Simon was nowhere to find. *Damn!* I had to act quickly. The tension in the air was so thick, you could slice through it with the edge of a piece of notebook paper.

Doubty took over my mind completely, paralyzing it with a flood of doubts. Perfecto, on the other hand, was hard at work rejecting any idea I came up with, convincing me that it wasn't good enough. *Have I taken too great a risk this time? Did I have too much faith in my ability to stop this conflict? What if my success thus far has just been beginner's luck? Perhaps it was only due to Simon's magic? And why, oh why, wasn't he showing up?*

I closed my eyes for a moment. I realized Simon wasn't coming to help me out this time. I was on my own. Even if he had come, he probably would've said something like, "It's not a complete disaster. This is an excellent opportunity to practice your art." *But what is an artist supposed to do in a case like this? What would Simon do if he were in my place?* What would you do?

* * * * *

"I'd be running away." Gill volunteered his answer.

"And everyone would remember you as a coward for the rest of your life," David said, releasing a knowing sigh that suggested he had tried it before.

Gill seemed to regret his quick answer. "Well, I didn't really mean that. I think I might try one of Simon's exercises. If it works with him there, it should also work when he isn't there, right?"

"Let's see," JJ said, using the moment to take another sip of cold water from his bottle.

* * * * *

I tried to visualize what would happen here if I didn't act quickly. A battle between two groups of children who are full of anger, fear and hatred, can get very ugly. Especially if those children are armed, trained to fight, and ready for battle. A chill trickled down my spine. When combatants stand in each other's way, the result is a war. This situation seemed impossible to resolve. The kids wouldn't listen to Simon's wisdom, even if I, a kid their age, was the one to share it with them. They'd laugh at me and then still attack each other. I needed to find a different solution.

I decided I might as well try one of Simon's exercises. I gave in to the situation and released the pressure. *I need to create the reality I choose*, I thought. I had to come up with a plan, overlook obstacles, and ignore Doubty and Perfecto. The fact that Simon wasn't coming to my rescue was probably part of another lesson. I thought about my confrontation with Rafael and Tom. Even if my attempt was going to fail in this case, the compassion concept was worth trying. There were two groups who wanted the same things: to sweat, run, release aggressions, and literally kick each other's asses. *Was fighting the only way to do that?*

"I bet we can beat you in a thirty-minute or five goal game. You guys don't have a chance against us," I said, slowly.

Silence swept over the field. Nobody moved. Weapons remained in the air, frozen in position. Kind of stunned and still undecided, everyone retained the option of starting a battle. Abby stopped his Nunchaku rotation. All eyes turned to me. I felt like a fan from the winning, visitor's team, accidentally caught in the middle of a group of angry fans from the defeated, home team.

I knew it wasn't going to succeed. Rafael gave me the same look that I give May after she does something really bad. It seemed like BJ was redirecting his assault target from Rafael to me. I had made a big mistake. *Why did I try to intervene? What was I thinking?* I wasn't a powerful magician, I was just an ordinary boy. BJ approached me and Rafael; his gang followed. I saw no choice but to fight in order to save myself. I tried to recall my Kung Fu moves, to plan out my first course of attack, but I couldn't remember anything. In all of the time I had spent with Simon, he had taught me only art, not combat skills.

Except for the small amount of training with Alon, I hadn't trained at all. I seemed to have forgotten everything.

BJ stood a 2x4's distance away from me and Rafael. He raised his wooden plank up in the air and I cringed, waiting for it to hit me. *If I survived*, I swore to myself, *I'd never get involved in conflicts like this ever again*. It was clear that I'd also never be an artist. Damn! I was just not artist material. I should stick to being a warrior like the rest of my friends; it was what I knew best. The warrior path was easier, even if it cost some bruises every once in a while.

I could smell BJ's sweat. It was mixed with the same kind of aftershave my dad used. I closed my eyes, desperately trying to surrender the fear that froze me. I heard the whir of a fast-moving 2x4 cut through the air. Then, BOOM! The board hit something. I opened one eye just a small crack to see what happened. *Was I hit?* I didn't feel any pain. *Am I dead?* I saw the 2x4 lying on the ground next to my feet. It had hit a rock, not me.

"You think you're so smart?" BJ asked. "We'll see who's going to have the last laugh. Let's play seven on seven. Whoever wins gets the field. You have no chance," he said, and then chuckled, his gang joining in a chorus of wicked laughter.

Rafael squeezed my shoulder and turned to point at Tom, Kid, Abbruce Lee and two other kids. "Let's beat them, boys," he said to us.

Yes! It worked. I was an artist! It's true, Doubty and Perfecto were close to taking over but, in the end, I handled the situation like an artist.

The game ended in a tie, 3-3. No team was able to defeat the other, even after a ten-minute overtime and some penalty kicks. However, we all had so much fun that BJ and Rafael scheduled a rematch for the next day. *Was this the beginning of a beautiful friendship?*

To my surprise, I wasn't in a celebrating mood. I didn't feel like a hero as I expected that I would. There was a heavy burden on my chest. I tried to understand what was wrong, but I couldn't. I decided to surrender. I released my thoughts, gave in to my senses, and let go of all resistance. I scanned my body again and came up with the sensations of fear and helplessness. I surrendered to these feelings, so I could connect to my emotions and experience them fully. After a moment, everything became clear. If there had actually been a fight with BJ's gang, I wouldn't have been ready, and they'd have mowed me down. "If I don't start to train again, I won't be ready for the next test," I told myself, in a worried voice.

"Which road are you walking now?" Guess who had just appeared out of nowhere, startling me when he spoke. After the game, I separated from the other kids. Without realizing where I was going since I was so deep in thought, my legs had carried me toward "our" park bench, just a ten-minute walk from the soccer field.

I turned to face Simon. He sat on the short grass; his legs bent back, his buttocks resting on his heels. "I… I'm walking the warrior path … the fear path, as you call it," I stammered. I hung my head in shame after updating him on the latest events and their effect on me.

"You have nothing to be ashamed of. You should be proud of yourself! You're practicing the artist path. Change comes with practice. This afternoon you were a great artist twice."

"Really? When?"

"First in the conflict, and then again when you identified and dealt with your fear. I'm so proud of you. Okay, so now you're experiencing a bit of a warrior state again but, as you already know, life is a never-ending process. Do you enjoy the path we're walking? Do you feel that you grow?"

"Yes, very much. I love the meetings with you. I learn a lot. I feel like I've found my own way on the artist path. I feel that I'm on the right track."

"So, forget the goal. If you walk toward the goal, you'll eventually achieve it, and if not, that's okay too. Just remember that we spend most of our lives on the path and only a short time at the destination; if you don't enjoy the path, you won't enjoy the majority of your life."

"Let me see if I understand," I said. "It's like my Green Belt experience. I trained for a year, that was the path, to get a belt, which was my goal. And if you really look at it, actually getting the belt is a 30-second long ceremony, right?"

He grinned. "I already told you that you have all the answers. If you don't enjoy the road you are traveling, you're not going to be happy. In addition, any path you walk changes you, it helps you to reveal more layers of your true self. The main value of goals isn't in achieving them, but in the person you become while working to achieve them. You must ask yourself, 'When I finally achieve this goal, will I feel happy with whom I'm going to be?'"

"I think I got it." I jumped on the bench. "The path I walk defines me at least as much as achieving the goal. For example, if I win a race by cheating, I'd probably not feel as good as if I got second place honestly."

"Excellent example. I need to remember it," he said, and looked like he was trying to push my example into his memory. "How many steps are there in one moment of a long journey?" This was an unexpected turn in his questioning.

"In one moment... I think there's only one step." It was the best guess I could make.

"Exactly," he said. "And the current moment is all we have. All previous moments are forever lost in the past; we can never return to them. All future moments are patiently waiting for us. We live only in the present, therefore the current step is all there is."

"But what if I'm hiking on a long road; then there's more than one step, right?"

"Not really. A long journey is just set decoration. Any step that you take carries within it every step that preceded it; it represents each step that led you to that point, everything that you've learned and everything that you've experienced. It also holds the power of the steps to come, which are determined by your direction at that moment in time."

"How exactly?"

"Are you studying agriculture at school?" he asked.

"Yeah. But what does that have to do with it?"

"The seeds you sow today determine what will grow from the ground tomorrow. It works in agriculture like it works with everything else in life."

"Okay, but how does all of this relate to me being unprepared for the Green Belt test?"

"Very simple. Pain and frustration are caused by resistance. Therefore, you should always accept the step you're taking, just as it is. Don't regret that you aren't taking, haven't taken, or won't take a different step. What you learn at this moment is what's right for you now."

"That reminds me," I said, "of a character on a children's show that always wanted to be 'there.' He kept trying to get 'there,' and everywhere he went, he asked, 'Am I there already?' Yet he kept hearing, 'No, you're here.'"

"You got it right. What exists is here and now, and if you don't accept that, you'll always be frustrated. You'll never be 'there.' Most people, especially youngsters, want to always be in 'tomorrow.' They think that everything will be much better in the future. Other people, usually the older folks, miss being in the 'yesterday.' They remember things as if they were much better in the past. But young or old, these people all have the same problem, they aren't satisfied with the here and now; they always want to be 'there'."

"I think you're right. That was exactly my problem with the Kung Fu trainings. I was impatient and tried to skip steps. I always wanted to be there. I've never been satisfied with the here and now. I see now that it was difficult for me to improve my skills having this mindset."

"Don't feel badly, this is the problem for most of us," he said. "Remember my rule about change and acceptance?"

I nodded.

"Well, after the conversations that we have had since, I think I'd like to add to it," he continued. "The extended version is, 'If I feel I want to be *there*, it means I'm not happy *here*. In this case I have three options," he began counting off on his fingers. "First, I can change *here* to suit me more. Second, I can go somewhere else, to another *here*, instead of looking for *there*. *There* is like tomorrow, it never comes. And the third option is to accept *here* as it is, surrender any negative judgments, and choose to enjoy the *here* and what it brings."

"I remember you told me about this rule. Resistance doesn't help, it only causes misery. But still, this rule is very confusing with all the here's and there's. I want to see if I understand it correctly, I'll use Kung Fu in my example. The Green Belt is equivalent to my *there*, and enjoying the training is equal to my *here*. I wanted so much to be *there*, that I gave up on being *here*. This is why I wasn't ready for the test. Does that make sense?"

"Yes, you got it."

"Okay, but can you please give me another example? I'm not sure that I know how to apply this to my normal life."

He smiled at me understandingly. "Suppose you want more peace and quiet inside your head. The search for this state of calm alone doesn't bring it. The search for inner peace, the 'there,' creates an internal struggle. It becomes a battle between 'I'm here' and 'I want to be there;' this brings even more frustration. Learn to forgive yourself for not always achieving a state of peace. Feel and accept the chaos or disruption, and suddenly you'll find that you have become calm."

I chuckled. "You never run out of examples, do you? I'll try it. Fighting the chaos doesn't exactly sound like a good plan. I mean, living a war can't bring peace."

"Excellent. Now we're getting to the interesting part of being an artist. The warrior tries to get what he thinks he deserves by fighting for it. This is his way. His goal is the only thing that matters and the path to achieve that goal is just a tool. He never accepts being here, he always wants to be there---"

"This reminds me of a western movie I watched." I interrupted him. "The cowboy hero was fighting evil villains throughout the entire movie; at the end of the movie, he won. But instead of staying in the town and enjoying his victory, he jumped on his loyal horse and galloped into the sunset as the movie credits rolled. I imagine that he was racing off in search of a new war to win. He was a warrior and that's what they do. Oops, sorry, you were in the middle of a sentence. Please continue."

He smiled indulgently. "A fine example. The artist avoids fighting as much as he can, while still working to achieve his goals. He doesn't wait for miracles, he produces them like a magician. An artist, as opposed to a warrior, is fully present and accepts the here and now. Now that you understand that, I think it's time for you to begin your Kung Fu training at the club again. You've almost completed your artist studies; it's time to start practicing the artist path in a new way, by implementing your skill into Kung Fu training."

The birds, who had blessed us with an *a cappella* performance, stopped singing. It seemed that even the wind stopped blowing in anticipation of my response. I couldn't find any words. At that moment, I felt like I was both the happiest and the saddest person in the whole world. I was an artist who had almost completed his training. There was cause to celebrate. Yet if I had almost achieved my goal, that meant that my journey was coming to an end.

I didn't know whether it was the joy or sadness that I was experiencing, but it felt as if the huge dam I had built to hold back my tears was threatening to crack. I imagined a trickle of tears flowing down my face. One after the other they'd say goodbye to my cheek before joyfully leaping toward my mouth, like paratroopers jumping from a plane. I could almost taste their pleasant saltiness. This was the closest I had come to tears in years, but still I couldn't cry. The damn dam remained strong. If I was able to cry, it'd have made a perfect moment.

"Our journey isn't over yet." Simon held my wrist reassuringly. "Don't worry, we still have a few more meetings."

"Thanks," I smiled weakly at him. That was the only way I could respond. The next day, I'd rejoin the Kung Fu club to continue with my training, this time as an artist. The color of my belt wasn't that important anymore, and as a result, it felt closer than ever.

Simon looked like a proud father watching his son climb another rung on the ladder of life. "I have something more for you, an exercise that will help with your training. If you practice it as much as possible, nothing will be able to stop you."

"I'm listening," I said, making sure he'd go on.

"Take deep breaths. Slowly fill your body with air, one organ at a time, until you can feel your body from within. Take notice of your ribs, moving up and down, while breathing. Listen to your heart beating. Look at the world through one eye, then through the other, then through both. Feel the earth beneath your feet. The touch of the air on your skin. Smell the air you inhale. Consciously breathe into each part of your body, and focus on the areas that are unwell, tensed, painful or loveless. Exhale the old energy, and allow fresh energy to fill your whole body, bit by bit."

A sour expression filled my face. I wasn't expecting this kind of exercise. I hoped for some fighting tips. "What is this exercise good for?"

"Being present within your body will help you to experience the here and now of every moment. A true artist is present during the time he spends on training, while he's fighting, and when he's resting. This consciousness and presence strengthens him."

"Oh. Okay, gotcha."

"Good. Meanwhile, I encourage you to practice another exercise. Feel yourself outside of your body; like a genie whose body was trapped in a bottle, but once freed, he has a huge energetic body. Get in touch with this out-of-the-bottle body. Become aware of other people and your connection with them. Focus on the world and its smells, colors and sounds. Turning your attention outward, calms the mind and liberates you. You'll be able to detect details that usually escape your notice. How can you stop and smell the flowers, if you're rushing around, busy thinking about what you have to do tomorrow?"

"Sounds interesting. Being present inside and outside. I'll try it." My initial disappointment was replaced with enthusiasm. "Am I supposed to practice both versions together?"

"I'd start to practice them separately, and only after you feel comfortable with each should you try them together. Each exercise has its own qualities; both exercises together have a totally different sensation. Try to feel the difference between them when you practice them separately. Then compare that experience to practicing them simultaneously, as one exercise. Practice them when walking, while in the shower, during conversations, standing in line at the grocery store; practice these exercises all of the time, anywhere you go, and whatever you do. Then, you'll always be present."

"Sounds good. Do you have a tip to make this exercise work faster?"

Simon looked at me in a way which hinted to me that I had slipped off the path with my question, but he simply smiled and said, "Surrender to the exercise, don't expect any results. Do it slowly and patiently. Pay attention to any emotion that arises, to any sensation inside or outside of the body. Try it once, and then try it again with less effort. Try to relax as much as you can. Take notice of where you struggle and then move on to a different area. The secret is to make it an effortless practice, then you'll have the best results. Have you ever seen an oak struggling to be a tree? Have you ever seen a small plant trying to speed up its growth process?"

I giggled as he turned away. "Why am I not surprised that this is your answer?" The very next minute, like a diligent student, I happily began to practice his most recent assignment.

22 - I WANT TO HEAR A STORY

When I rejoined my group at the dojo most of the kids already had Green Belts or higher. It surprised me, but I didn't feel that they were any better or worse than me just because I still had a yellow belt. I simply practiced being an artist at every opportunity. I felt much lighter during my trainings this time around, and I advanced faster than ever. Simon was right; it was much easier to learn Kung Fu when I walked the artist path. I also improved my soccer skills by playing like an artist. When the new school year started, I'd apply the artist practice to my studies; I bet this would make my classes easier too.

    I particularly liked the last trick that Simon had taught me about being aware and present. While walking up the shaded hill to the dojo, I practiced being aware of myself and what was taking place both inside and outside of my body. I liked to begin my practice of feeling present in my tail bone. I concentrated all of my attention on my lower back, and then raised my focus and traveled up my spine to my skull. I was my spine. I felt long and straight. Sometimes I practiced being present through one of my ears. The world sounds quite different from there. Other times I tried to perceive the world and my place in it from a toe, my lungs, or my heart. Each part of my body that I visited got full attention before I moved on to the next part. I repeated this until I had "visited" and then felt present throughout my body.

I talked to my internal organs and gave them warmth and love. At the same time, I practiced feeling outside of my body. I assimilated the signals that my senses gathered from the external world. Before this exercise my life looked like a low resolution movie on *YouTube*. After practicing it, my life seemed like a Blu-ray movie on an HD screen. The world spoke to me, and I enjoyed a feeling of presence that I hadn't known before.

Another few weeks passed and the school year began. There were new teachers, new friends and new classes. Alisa was now old enough to attend school. Every morning I greeted her with the question, "Who's a school girl?" In response, she smiled proudly, inflating her cheeks. One morning I watched her organize rainbow-colored pencils, exotically scented erasers and other supplies in her backpack. *What a little artist*, I thought. She's sculpting with school stuff. Too bad she doesn't know Simon... Hmmm, Simon... I haven't heard from him for several weeks. Truthfully, I started to miss him.

Later that day May and I went out for a stroll in the park. May dragged me to her favorite maple tree. While she dug a hole in the muddy ground beneath the tree, I watched a group of girls from my class that were playing some girly game on one of the park's basketball courts. Of course, no one knew that I had a secret crush on one of them. I was working up my courage to go and talk to her, when I sensed someone standing behind me.

"Hello, Simon," I said, as I turned to face him. He hadn't surprised me this time. Through awareness of my body and what was present outside of it, I had become more conscious. An artist's smile covered my face. He tipped his straw hat at me in a gesture of recognition of my new ability.

"I see that you don't need me as a teacher anymore. You can discover everything for yourself now. Well done!" He sounded pleased.

"But I'm not done yet. Please don't leave me! Don't you have anything else to teach me? I love the meetings we have. Come on, I want another lesson." I was prepared to beg if I had to.

He put his hand on my shoulder. "I'm not leaving yet, don't worry. But today we aren't going to learn anything since I have nothing new to teach you. We're just going to spend the afternoon together. What would you like to do? What do you love to do but haven't done for a long time?"

He caught me off guard with another one of his weird questions. "I don't know. Between school, friends, Kung Fu and soccer, which have all become routine, I don't have time to think about other activities that I like. Let's see. What have I forgotten about that I enjoy or haven't had the time for?" I racked my brain and couldn't come up with anything. I decided to use the surrendering exercise. I gave up on the need to have an answer, closed my eyes, and just imagined myself as happy. A wave of joy came over my body and a pleasant sensation bristled through my hair.

I opened my eyes and looked at Simon and May. May sat watching me and seemed to smile. "Of course, how come I didn't think of this before? May is the universe's greatest happiness expert. Let's follow her lead and take a walk without having a destination. Let's stop and smell the wind, listen to far away sounds, and enjoy the scenery. Let's find things that we aren't looking for. I haven't done that in years. Actually, I don't even remember the last time I did it. Maybe when I was Alisa's age. It's so much fun. That's what I want to do today!" I was pleased with my own answer. Simon had tricked me. Even though he said that he was teaching nothing, I was learning from him. It reminded me of our lesson on nothing which is really something.

While we walked, time ceased to exist. I gazed at the ancient clock, standing atop the tower in the city's central square. It looked back at me in despair. If someone were to ask what time it was, at that moment, there was only one possible answer, "Now!" After all, what other time could it be?

"At moments like this," Simon said, "you can see that time really isn't moving, it's still. We keep progressing forward toward the future, so we mistakenly perceive time as moving backwards, taking away sixty more seconds of our lives, in each new minute. One has to stop and reflect in order to see it."

I diligently practiced being present and conscious of both my inside and outside worlds while we walked. I had walked this trail many times before on my way to school. I thought there was nothing I hadn't seen there before. I was wrong. It started with a quiet tweeting sound from the smiling tree. It came from a sparrows' nest up in its branches that I had never noticed before. A sudden salty wind slapped my cheek. I looked to the right and saw the sea peeking through the buildings. I didn't know you could see the sea from this place. Then intoxicating scents caught my attention. They were coming from the various tulips growing in the building's yards and from flowering vines climbing the fences.

After hours of walking which seemed like only moments, I realized that we had hiked to the top of the highest hill in town. A vast field of buildings lay spread below our feet, encircled by the sea to the west and the lowlands and mountains to the east. I could see traces of the pleasant west wind gently brushing the leaves on the trees as it traveled, from sea to mountains, across the land.

"Let's sit here and rest for a bit," Simon offered, pointing to a bench. "I'm tired from all the walking."

I knew he wasn't really tired. He was being considerate of how I may have been feeling. May didn't lose a second and immediately lay down. I stroked her gently and looked at Simon. "Tell me a story! No one has told me one for years and I miss it so much. Dad is too busy for stories, and Mom thinks I'm too old for that."

Sometimes I think Mom doesn't know me at all. "My little Ehudi fears elevators, hates magicians and loves cabbage," I lately heard her telling Aunt Hannah. It was true, I'd rather take the stairs, but I don't fear elevators. I saw a magician perform once and didn't like it, but he was pretty bad. And cabbage? It's gross. I was disgusted at the very thought of it. How did she come up with these ideas?

I joined Simon on the bench and watched the far waves in the sea. "Listening to a story is something else that I enjoy but haven't done for a long time. Would you please tell me one?"

Simon winked at me. "What are the odds? I just happened to have thought of a story to tell you. Are you ready?"

I checked on May. She was lying on her side with her tongue hanging out. She must have been pooped after the long hike. She wouldn't object to a story if it allowed her more time to rest. "Of course I'm ready!"

23 - WHAT IF EVERYTHING WAS TRANSPARENT?

"My story is about a boy who made an unbelievable difference in his tribe just by presenting his people with a new perspective," Simon began. "It took place a thousand years ago, in a place called *The Land of the Great Mud River*, home of the *High Feathers* tribe. High Feathers was a peaceful tribe, yet its warriors, especially the chief, *Running with Horses*, were the bravest in the land. Running with Horses' courage and kindness were known across more land than an eagle can cover flying continuously for a full moon cycle.

On the longest day of each year, the High Feathers tribe observed its ancient custom of holding a rite of passage ceremony. All the boys who had seen 13 summers celebrated their passage from childhood to adulthood and became warriors. Beginning on the night of the last full moon before the ceremony, the warriors who had seen 31 summers mentored the boys and taught them to fight, hunt, and participate in various men's chores."

A couple, holding hands, passed by our bench and greeted us. May raised her head, stretched her legs and sighed. She licked my bare foot once and put her head between her paws. I chuckled and nodded for Simon to continue.

"During the seven moons before the ceremony, the soon-to-be celebrated children would demonstrate their knowledge of skills, like signaling with fire and reading trails. Once a boy passed every trial, he was given an ax, a knife, and a bow. With these tools, he was expected to make arrows and hunt for the food to be served at the ceremonial dinner.

This ceremony was one of the greatest festivals of the year. The warriors wore their war costumes, while the elders and women wore festival regalia. When the moon reached the center of the sky, the drummers began to beat their instruments slowly, the woodwind musicians joined in with their cheerful sounds, and everyone began to dance. As the drummers beat their instruments louder and faster, everybody raised their hands to the sky and began to sing the rite of passage songs. Their voices were so harmonious and loud that, according to the legend, the spirits of the dead rose up from the earth and soared like eagles above the celebration.

After thirteen rounds of song and dance, the shaman of the tribe stood before the boys and their mentors and sang a peace prayer over them. Then the veteran warriors, who had mentored the boys, passed their own weapons on to the new warriors. From that moment, the veteran warriors were no longer combatants. Now they'd have a new role as men of peace. It had already been this way for thousands of moons, when the time came time for *Walking on Clouds* to make his transition from boyhood to manhood.

Walking on Clouds had always been unlike the other children. He hadn't yet seen his fifth winter when, one windy morning, he climbed atop a tree stump seat in the center of the noisy children's tent. As skinny and short as he was, it took a few minutes before the kids took notice of his waving hands. Facing them he asked, 'What if everything was transparent?'

The tent grew quiet. The youngest didn't understand the question. The older children weren't sure of the answer. The adult caretakers stopped what they were doing and stared at Walking on Clouds. He provided a simple answer to his own question, 'There would be no more curious people.'

There was an ancient tale, passed from father to son, prophesying that one day *The Artist* would come to the people of High Feathers. The Artist would have the ability to see through things, and he would one day change the world's order, until the heavens came down and the earth rose up. Could it be that Walking on Clouds was the artist of legend? Walking on Clouds seemed an appropriate name for someone who would make the sky his land."

I tried to hold back from saying something, but I couldn't do it. "I already love this kid," I said. Simon grinned and continued.

"Those who heard about what had transpired in the children's tent were fascinated by the wisdom of Walking on Clouds. From that day forward, many called him The Artist.

This boy continued to amaze everyone time after time, but the culmination came several moons before the longest day of the thirteenth summer of his life. On that night, he notified his father that he did not wish to become a warrior. He declared that he felt ready to join the men of peace. His father couldn't comprehend how his son could have such an unwise desire. He thought perhaps that, as the sun and moon rotated and the other boys trained with their warrior mentors, logic might prevail and Walking on Clouds would reconsider. However, as the other boys learned the ways of the warrior, he didn't join them. The disappointed father couldn't look at his son anymore. He wished what was happening was just a bad dream. Eventually he saw no option but to raise the issue with the tribesmen.

The next day, same as every evening at dusk, the chief, Running with Horses came to the village center, lit a fire, and sat at the northernmost point of the circle. His black eyes stared at the skies and his muscular body froze, as he thought deeply about what to say. Soon after, the tribe's warriors joined him at his right, while the tribe's elders - the men of peace, sat at his left. Each group formed a semicircle, together completing a full circle around the bonfire. To mark the beginning of the meeting, Running with Horses raised his left hand and lit the *calumet*, the peace pipe. He inhaled its smoke, and exhaled into the center of the circle. It was believed that, through the calumet, one drew in the smoke of peace, and released the smoke of war. Walking on Clouds, who was invited to the meeting for the first time, was ordered to take a seat between the elders and the warriors.

Running with Horses started to speak. 'My dear peace keepers and warriors, I need your advice. Tomorrow, as everyone knows, is supposed to be a particularly special celebration day for me. It's the time that my eldest son, Walking on Clouds, is to transition from boy to warrior.'

He bit his lip and continued. 'However, much to my dismay, he has chosen not to participate in the warrior testing. He believes that he will be 31, not 13. He has expressed his desire to join the tribe's men of peace. Our ancient rule is that a boy who refuses to become a warrior must be expelled from the tribe forever. Such a refusal has never happened before. Although he has the chance to change his mind by tomorrow, I know him well, and I feel this will not happen. He has always been unlike the others. I have tried, for many seasons, to reform his ways with no success. Maybe it's because I'm not a good father. Before I banish him from our tribe, I seek your wise advice.'

Some sighs went around the circle. The men were stunned by the chief's words. No one dared to speak, since no one could think of what to say. The silence lasted a long time. Finally, the unhappy chief made himself ready to announce his verdict. As sad as it made him, he knew that he had no choice.

But then an elder signaled that he wished to speak. His name was *Seeing Far* and he was considered one of the wisest people ever born into the tribe. He rarely spoke but, when he opened his mouth, even the crickets respectfully stopped their noises to listen. The pipe was passed to Seeing Far; he inhaled, exhaled, and began to speak.

'Honorable chief, respected sages, and brave warriors—no one here today has seen more sunsets than I. I have seen great warriors come and go. I have seen mighty blizzards and blinding sand storms. I have seen years of plenty and years of deadly famine. One might think I have seen everything. But this boy is like none other that I have ever seen. I have been waiting for his emergence all of my days. I thought that perhaps, as the years progressed, *The Artist* would not appear in this life cycle. I thank Great Spirit for not taking me back before he emerged. It is my request that we listen with open hearts to his reasons before we decide his future.'

Murmurs of approval went around the circle and the calumet made its way to The Artist.

The child inhaled its smoke, coughed, exhaled, cleared his throat and began to speak. 'Kind father, respected sages, and fearless warriors—tomorrow is supposed to be the biggest day of my life, I am supposed to transition from a child to a fighting man. For the next eighteen years I am supposed to contribute as a warrior, serving my tribe to protect my people. It has been our way as far back as we can remember. But I see what is needed with different eyes. I believe that in every man's life there are three stages.

The first: that of childhood. This is where the boy acquires skills that will prepare him to take the next step. During childhood, life seems to revolve around the boy, at least from his viewpoint. The adults help him, and he enjoys playing as he slowly grows and learns.

In the next stage, the boy becomes a man, a warrior. He learns to fight for his needs, and is willing to die protecting his honor, his family and his people. At this stage he discovers that being a hard worker is what it takes to find success.

When he reaches the last stage, he has already achieved almost everything he wanted. Now his real contribution to the tribe begins. He has trained in the ways of war, and therefore can appreciate the ways of peace. He has learned to work with nature, not against it. This is his time to help raise our children.' Walking on Clouds stopped speaking for a moment and looked around the circle; all eyes were focused on him. He continued.

'Many moons ago, someone decided upon an appropriate time for these two important stages to begin. Have you ever asked yourself why that particular age was selected? Is it still right for us? Is it enough to say that it is right just because we have always done it this way? Do we all have children born to us at the same age? Are we all equally strong? Do we all live to see the same number of seasons as our neighbor?'

He took a deep breath. 'We each have our own pace: we are a child, a warrior, and eventually a man of peace for a different length of time. Let us accept this. Let us allow each child to choose when he wants to become a warrior. Let us also support the warrior's decision about when he wants to pass on his weapons. Maybe the warrior is ready to progress to the next stage after fifteen hunting seasons, maybe after forty. Let us not let the old way determine the future. I understand that tradition, customs and wisdom are important and help guide us, but when we look at Mother Earth, we can see that even the mighty river changes its course over time. Even mighty stones crumble to dust under the touch of the wind. Earth herself changes, sometimes before the eyes of men.'

Walking on Clouds surveyed the faces around the fire. He looked at the elders; they looked back at him, their faces seeming to say that they were in agreement. However, as he had expected, his father and the warriors looked quite doubtful. Combatants tend to defend their beliefs because they fear any change that may threaten their steadfast answers. It's difficult to offer a new way of doing things against such a resistant force. The boy remembered back to when his father once told him, 'A person usually will not remember what you said, but will always remember how you made him feel.' Walking on Clouds knew that, in order for his message to be accepted, he should help the others feel his words.

He continued his speech. 'We live in an illusion. If you look at this mirage of life from another viewpoint, it may become clear to you. Take my father, for instance. For you, he is the chief, the hero warrior. For me, he is a loving, protective father, a source of wisdom and inspiration. In the eyes of our neighboring tribes, he is a dangerous and relentless enemy who is frightening to encounter in battle. The beauty of illusion is that we all see the same thing in a different way.

We are all parts of Great Spirit, who is perfect. In order to experience its own perfection, Great Spirit split into many small pieces--more than the number of the stars in the sky. Each one of us is a piece, wearing our own shape and choosing a unique point of view. The combination of these infinite points of view enables Great Spirit to experience life from every angle.'

An eagle cried out in the distance. Walking on Clouds paused for a moment, listening. He stared at the far away, white topped mountains and deeply inhaled their energy.

'Take, for example, the black panther. It is all black, like a moonless cloudy night. A night which makes you feel like there is nothing in the darkness that surrounds you. But the world is still out there, and the brave ones can find the best hunts on moonless nights. The darkness, where nothing is known, is the place to find answers, to connect to the real forces within our world, and to find the light of hidden truth. That is why the panther is the smartest predator on our land.

We have forgotten our source, so we will be able to experience the illusion created for us. Now imagine a giant field crowded with tiny pieces of spirit. Each one has a different view of the world.

The warrior believes that in order to change his viewpoint, he has to change his physical place. To do this, he feels someone must change places with him. He is stubborn, persistent, and ready to do anything and lose everything just to achieve the goal. Living within that perspective is how conflicts and wars come about. This comes from the belief that if I am strong, someone has to be weak; if I win, someone else must lose.

Deep down inside, the sage feels that he lives in a mirage. He understands that his reality is created through his perception, and therefore a change does not have to be physical. A sage believes that the world is made up of his sisters and brothers, whether they are people, animals or aspects of nature. For these are all tiny pieces of

Great Spirit. We are all fingers of the same hand. When a sage wants to see things from a particular point of view, all he has to do is to sit quietly, close his eyes and imagine himself in the new spot.

The warrior does not believe this is possible. His attention is on separation, not on unity. The sage has no doubts, and knows how to see through the illusion into the darkness on the other side. He dismantles his resistance and experiences the obstacles that are, really, of his own creation. By experiencing these obstacles and working through them, he makes them disappear. Then he raises his head and notices another neighbor spirit who wants to change its point of view. For every one that wants to go in one direction, there is always another one who wants to go in the opposite direction. That is how the perfection is maintained.'

The young boy stood up and raised his hands to the sky. 'What distinguishes a sage from a warrior is not age, but the understanding that a change in perception is more powerful than any physical change. Everyone has a different perspective, whether he is a wise elder or a young warrior. All angles are important and are necessary to maintain the balance of the Great Spirit. Someone has to be considered wrong, so that someone else can be considered right. The contrasts between us create the perfection of Great Spirit.'

Walking on Clouds shook with excitement. He had exposed a great truth and, in doing so, agitated his audience. He hadn't thought about what he would say before he began speaking. Great Spirit intervened, giving the illusion that Its words were those of Walking on Clouds. This was Great Spirit's way of experiencing perfection.

A light, warm, eastern wind blew some tumbleweed a few inches above the heads of the men seated around the bonfire. It was the only sound that could be heard at that moment. No one moved or motioned for the calumet. The chief looked at his son with an expression that mixed sadness and pride. A few minutes later, after all the men had had an opportunity to think about what had been said, they began to request the calumet and a long discussion about the boy's speech followed. Some agreed with him and others stuck to their ancestors' wisdom. They tried to sway each other for hours until pale rays of sun appeared in the east. Finally it was voted to adopt the boy's suggestions.

From that day forward, every boy in the village could choose for himself the appropriate age when he would leave childhood and become a warrior. Similarly, every warrior could decide upon the age when he would pass on his weapons and become a man of peace.

Each year, on the day before the longest day, there was a special meeting at dusk. After the chief seated himself, all of the proud males who chose to be warriors for the next four seasons seated themselves to his right. Some of these males were children who sat there for the first time; others were veteran warriors, who had sat to the right of the chief for many hunting seasons. To the chief's left sat the wise elders and the proud males who chose to become men of peace.

On the next day, the men both young and old of the High Feathers tribe would announce how they would make their best contribution. Some of those who had wanted to shift their role and change their place around the fire the day before, would realize that they were not really ready. They had thought it was time to change, but realized they were mistaken. They would remain in their previous role. This was done without shame as these men had discovered that their time to change had still not arrived. They could always make the shift in the coming seasons.

The tribal men learned that child, warrior, and man of peace were all just states of consciousness; each would experience these states at his own pace."

* * * * *

"What happened with the boy?" I asked Simon.

"At the end of that meeting, he mounted his pony and left the tribe. He completed his duty, shifted his people's attitude and felt the call to serve as an ambassador of change to help others. It is said that from that day on, he wandered around the world teaching the artist path. Some say that he's still around bringing awareness to people."

ONE-LEGGED SEAGULL

May released a sigh, rose from the ground and stretched her hind legs. She knew that the end of a story is always the beginning of something else.

24 - IT'S A JUNGLE OUT THERE, NOT A SCHOOL PLAYGROUND

"I loved Simon's story," Gill said, with a big smile. "*The Artist* was really something special, huh? I mean, convincing the tribesmen to change their perspective after so many years is huge!" He glanced meaningfully at his parents. "And you know what? I've discovered that I have more in common with Ehud than I originally thought. Just like him, I don't like school; it's a big effort. My problem is that I can't concentrate because I always think something more interesting is going on somewhere else. I want to be *there*. If I train like Ehud, there's a chance I might improve."

JJ seemed pleased. "I'm glad to hear that."

"The idea of surrendering," Gill continued, "is totally new to me, but it seems that Ehud uses it in every possible way and gets good results. I'll practice Simon's exercises as well."

"Excellent."

"I think I could be friends with Ehud if I knew him. It was an excellent idea to tell us this story."

"Stop, stop, I'm blushing." JJ said, winking.

Sara nestled deeper into the sofa, her hands stretched to the sides. "At school, I'm going to teach my students to become artists. The exercise of compassion... my life would be much easier if only my students would learn it. They can get really mean sometimes."

David's foot bounced nervously on the floor and his fingers tapped on his forehead. "I don't understand your enthusiasm. It's just a fairytale. What? Do you think if I surrendered or practiced compassion at work, it would change anything? They'd have me for lunch! It's a jungle out there, not a school playground. You show a weakness, and you become the prey. This is exactly what happened to me. Believe me. There's one guy in my office, Danny Cordova, he's so evil. You just can't see him any other way. In short, all of these exercises might be suitable for children, but they'd never work for me."

Gill and Sara looked stunned at David's outburst, but JJ wasn't surprised at all. He didn't expect the group's most experienced warrior to give up on his war so easily. JJ's long warrior past had taught him what to expect. Sometimes, JJ himself deviated from the artist path and reverted to his old ways for a short time. JJ did expect David to at least identify a bit with the chief character in the story though. He hoped that David would recognize that he too could be hard on his son sometimes, trying to force Gill to walk his father's path.

Sara attempted to chip away at her husband's firm position. "Dave, perhaps you should try to understand some of it. You forget that Doubty, who JJ, I mean Simon, mentioned, also caused you great damage at work. You didn't believe you were good enough for the new position. You gave up without even trying; this made it easy for Mr. Cordova to steal your promotion."

"Don't start with your nonsense again, Sary." David punched a pillow. "You know it infuriates me when you ramble on about subjects you know nothing about. Whether I believed in myself or not, it wouldn't have changed a thing."

Sara looked offended. "Shoot me, why don't you? I'm just trying to help you and this is how you repay me. Did you see that, JJ?"

"Ceasefire!" JJ cried out. "Don't you want to hear the end of the story?"

"Yes, Uncle, get on with the story. I'm dying to know if Ehud will finally pass the test. I also want to know what the deal is with Simon. How is he connected to Ehud? I have my suspicions, but I'll let you tell us because I don't want to ruin any surprise endings. Besides, I can listen to Mom and Dad fighting whenever I want to, at home."

"Ouch!" David took a deep breath. "You sucker punched me below the belt! Is that what I taught you?" He mussed up Gill's hair and put his arm around Sara. "Okay, so I didn't understand the story; no need to fight about it, right? Go on JJ. The Sabbath starts soon and my stomach is beginning to growl."

Sara laughed nervously, putting her hand on David's knee. "This one over here, as quickly as he blows up, is as quickly as he calms down. But if this story doesn't end soon, it looks like you're gonna be in big trouble, my dear brother."

JJ grinned. "I don't want to upset your stomach, David, so I'm continuing." *One thing is for sure, it never gets boring with them around*, he thought.

25 - THE DIARY

About a week before my Green Belt test, we practiced kumite, the one-on-one exercises, at the dojo. While I fixed my belt, everyone paired up quickly and I didn't have a partner. I looked toward the wooden benches by the main door to see if there were any late comers when I spotted Tom. He was standing at the edge of the mats, bowing toward the coach, asking for permission to join our practice.

Although we were no longer enemies, somehow in the ring we weren't exactly friends either. It was almost like he was eager to prove that he was a better fighter than me. A kumite with him was similar to a game between Maccabi and Hapoel in Tel Aviv, or like a game between the Mets and the Yankees in New York. No matter how the game went, how many points were scored, or what impressive moves were made, victory was ultimately the only thing that mattered.

We bowed to one another and the kumite began. We circled each other, careful not to get hurt while continuously looking for a way to break the opponent's defense. Thanks to my meetings with Simon and the training at the club that followed, I had turned into a much better Kung Fu artist. Tom was still quicker than me though, and the precision of his right-legged kicks was lethal.

While searching for his weak point, my glance passed over the Green Belt around his waist. Suddenly I saw all the Green Belts on the other kids that practiced around us. It upset me because it reminded me of my failure. Madly, I sent a kick to his stomach which almost cost me my balance, as Tom skillfully responded with a combined course of defense and attack. I jumped back and avoided his leg a split second before he would've made contact. I called a short break, saying I needed to fix my suit.

I had let anger hinder my performance. Luckily, for months I had practiced the ability to surrender unwanted emotions. I used the break to let go of my resistance. I gave in completely to my upset and deliberately experienced it. I felt my way through the blinding anger that overcame me. After amplifying the anger and expanding it to its edges, it was gone and I felt lighter.

I indicated to Tom that I was ready to begin again. We got into position. I reminded myself that I was an artist and let the feel of it fill me. While blocking Tom's attempt to kick me, I saw in my head a mental picture of one of my favorite moves. Most of the kids in my group knew it, but Tom hadn't yet joined us when the coach had taught it. I knew it'd surprise him.

I changed my hand positions, exposing my chest for an attack. Tom immediately recognized the opportunity and threw a punch at my chest. I responded quickly, abruptly kicking my left foot diagonally, up and out. I managed to drop off Tom's radar for an instant. One moment I was directly in front of him, at his height, and after my move, I had dropped to the floor on his right. His hand remained suspended in the air, where my chest had been just a fraction of a second before. I grabbed his right knee, my left hand pushing right and the right one pushing left. His leg bent, he lost his balance and tumbled to the mats. With the agility of a tiger I jumped on him, pinned him to the ground, and marked a strike to his face, as we don't really punch each other's faces in the dojo. Then I flashed a victory smile at the coach. I was ready for the test. Not only did I have a quick win, but it was against Tom and his Green Belt!

Tom took this defeat pretty hard. The second that training was over for the day, he hurried to change his clothes and left the dojo. I noticed that, probably due to his rush, he forgot his school bag under the bench by his locker. I decided to take it with me and return it to him or leave it by his front door on my way home. I put on my backpack and held his in my hands. I left the dojo to the dark street. While passing below a streetlamp I noticed that Tom's bag was unzipped. Something green peeked out through the opening. At first, I thought it was his belt which I wanted to see up close. I put my hand inside the bag to pull it out. It was a green notebook.

I thought back to the day when we collided in the hallway at school. I remembered how scared he was when he thought I was going to pick up that notebook. He was a total weirdo about having me see what was in that book. I had to find out the story behind it. Its cover didn't reveal any secrets, but when I opened it, the first page made everything clear. "Tom's Diary - Top Secret! Whoever dares to touch this notebook is risking his head!" Drawings of skulls and the word "death" scattered all over the page made it clear that no one other than Tom should read this diary.

Interesting, I thought. A diary seemed like something a kid way more sensitive than Tom would keep. I put it back in his bag without reading it. I decided to return it to Tom. It was important for me to respect his privacy.

The walk home seemed endless and my legs became increasingly heavy. I could think about only one thing, Tom's diary. The trees, buildings and street-signs, all seemed to point at the bag and whisper, "Ehud ... What did he write about you?" With much difficulty, I resisted the temptation to rip open Tom's bag and read through his diary. I tried to run and to ignore the temptation.

"*Read* it, kid," a tall old man, who I almost bumped into, said. I looked at him surprised. "You almost *read* into me. You have to *read* where you go."

That's it, I thought. I'm starting to hallucinate. If I don't read this diary I'm going to lose it. I found a good hiding spot behind some tall bushes in a building's yard and sat down. I tried one last time to surrender the curiosity. I felt through the uncontrolled need and amplified it. It was gone, for a few seconds, but then it took over again. I guess more artist training was needed, but in the meantime I pulled the diary out of Tom's bag and a flashlight out of mine. I began to thumb through it, looking for a specific date. I was dying to know what Tom had written about our collision in the school hallway. They say that curiosity killed the cat, but I bet the cat thought the risk was worth it. So did I.

* * * * *

Dear Diary, Another horrible day in my shitty life! It started when I got my final report card. Mrs. Gendler said that she was disappointed in me and wanted to speak with my parents. She said I'm very talented, and it's a shame that I'm wasting my talent and not focusing on school. Who does she think she is? I told her that she should go fuck herself. She got really mad. Her face turned red, and I swear there was smoke coming out of her ears. Who exactly am I supposed to bring to her? Dad? Lol... I asked her when she expected me to study- when I help Rafael at the gas station or when I clean the dojo? She said she wouldn't make it any easier on me, because that would mean she gave up on me just like everyone else. What's up with her? I don't want anything from her but to be left alone. Bitch!

In short, she was totally angry and sent me to the principal. I went to look for Rafael. I ran toward his classroom and BOOM! Ehud, that sissy kid, jumped out of nowhere and pushed me to the floor. If I had been ready, he'd have had no chance with me; but he surprised me. I made a Kung Fu jump from the floor back to my feet. I'd have killed him, if I hadn't been in trouble already. I warned him that Rafael would take care of him. He almost shit in his pants, that geek. He begged me to forgive him. I just laughed at him. There's no way he's gonna get away with this one! He deserves what he'll get, the little bugger. He's so pompous. He always walks around telling everyone how perfect he is, what a good student and a glorious Kung Fu warrior he is. That he's right-handed while his family is left-handed. What a bunch of crap! I was so thrilled when he failed the Green Belt test, that little shit. He thinks he deserves everything, that he's better than Rafael and me because of his great family. What a skunk.

I couldn't find Rafael and I was too upset, so I ran home. Mom was there. She probably just returned from the beauty salon and stopped at home to make us dinner before she goes to her second job. She wore sunglasses again. I bet to hide another black eye. Like I don't know. I didn't want to bother her about it, so I just pretended that everything was normal. It doesn't matter anyway. Even if I did ask her, I know she'd make up a story about walking into a closet door or something. Closet door my ass! I know exactly who beat her up. I lied and told her that everything was fine at school, so as not to drag her down any more. She has enough trouble without me.

When Rafael came home from school, we ate silently and then went to work at the gas station. He was nervous, probably because of Mom's eye, but maybe he also had problems at school. I didn't tell him what happened with Mrs. Gendler or Ehud, so I wouldn't upset him even more. As we were walking home past the bar where all Dad's loser, unemployed friends are "searching" for new jobs, Dad showed up there too. He asked Rafael for money to buy flowers for Mom. What a liar! Rafael told him that if he wants money, he should go to work like us. Then we both ran away fast before he could beat us too. God, what did we do to deserve this? Why couldn't I be born to a family like Ehud's? There's no justice in this whole damn world!

* * * * *

I was shocked. I never imagined that this is what went on with Tom and Rafael. From Tom's angle everything looked so different than it did from mine. I never knew that he was so jealous of me and my family. I felt feelings of compassion well up inside me for Tom,

Rafael, and their mom. Feeling compassion, which after much practice came more naturally to me, helped me cope with this new information. I was embarrassed by how I had judged them before, but I knew that berating myself wouldn't solve anything. I had already learned my lesson. If you look at life from only one viewpoint, you don't get a full picture because you miss all the other viewpoints. If I focus only on what I've done wrong, I'll miss the lesson when new information comes along. I promised myself to try and practice more compassion. I didn't want to repeat this mistake with anyone else.

I went back to the dojo and handed Tom's bag to our coach who was getting ready to leave. I told him that I thought it was Tom's, and that I found it in the dressing room. I preferred that he return it. I knew if I returned it, Tom would suspect that I had read his diary. I didn't want to look in his eyes and lie to him. I never mentioned this event to anyone, but it changed the way I looked at other people forever.

26 - IN OKINAWA, BELT MEAN, "NO NEED ROPE TO HOLD UP PANTS"

My Green Belt test was just around the corner, but time crept by like a wounded turtle. I walked between the living room and the kitchen restlessly, like a hungry lion pacing its cage. I needed to find some activities to distract me. I was confident in my ability to get to the Green Belt level, but I was filled with excess energy and emotions.

"What's on your mind, Ehudik?" Mom asked. "Why don't you go out and play ball or something?" Apparently, my restlessness worried her so much that she even forgot to ask about homework. "By the way, Aunt Hannah called this morning. She wanted to invite you to join her and the children to see 'Sean the Illusionist'. I told her that you probably wouldn't want to go since you don't like magicians."

"Mom!" I shouted loudly, in a whiney voice. "How many times do I have to tell you? Cabbage, I hate it! I'm not afraid of elevators and I love magicians! Call her back right away. I'm dying to see this magician!" *A magic show, to distract my thoughts from the test, is exactly what I need right now*, I thought. On her way to the phone, Mom muttered something about the cabbage pie that I used to love as a toddler and how I always seemed to pick the stairs over the elevator. She called Aunt Hannah and asked her to get me a ticket for the show.

* * * * *

Sean the Illusionist wore a black suit. His brown hair was slicked smoothly back like a 1950's rocker. He mesmerized us with his piercing eyes and mysterious voice. My cousins and I had front row tickets just by the edge of the stage, which made everything look even more real. The magician performed all of the usual magic tricks, like correctly guessing cards, making doves appear out of nowhere and pulling rabbits out of a hat, but he also performed tricks that I had never seen before. He turned two coins into three just by rubbing them together quickly. He made people think about a number that he had selected. He touched one person's hand while another person felt that touch.

Out of nowhere, my nerdy cousin, Josh, burst into tears. He was only six months younger than me, but he barely reached my shoulders. He was thin and his eyes bulged so much, it looked like they might pop out of his face, like a cartoon character.

Sean stopped the show and turned to Josh, "Why are you crying, bud?"

"I'm afraid of wizards," Josh whined. "Please don't bewitch me."

Sean chuckled. "I'm not a wizard, and I'm not going to harm anyone." He told us everything he did was just an illusion - a trick. He had only made us believe that he had hidden powers. Each of his stunts had a simple explanation. He even demonstrated one of the simplest tricks. He showed us how he had hidden a coin between his fingers in advance so it would appear that he had turned two coins into three. It made me think about what was real in the world. I mean, anything can be an illusion, a trick prepared ahead of time...

* * * * *

"And what if I imagined you, what if you're just my own illusion?" I asked Simon, when I spotted him the next day. He was waiting in line at a register in the candy store. It was just one day before the test. "What if everything you told me," I lowered my voice after a big lady with a small girl gave me a funny look, "from the first meeting to the last one, was an invention of your imagination and nothing was actually true?"

I had come a long way since the first Green Belt test. It hadn't been six months since that day, both the saddest and happiest day of my life. I was more confident. I enjoyed walking the artist path and practicing Simon's exercises. I gained the respect of my coach, my teammates, and the kids with higher belts. No one understood this sudden change within me; I couldn't explain it to them. What was I supposed to tell them? That after my failure, an old Tiberiaser named Simon Master appeared in my life and taught me that Kung Fu is an art, not a fight? They'd think I lost it.

Doubts about Simon and his path crept into my head. Doubty may have lost some battles, but he had no intention of being defeated completely or disappearing altogether. I had learned a lot from Simon, yet I still doubted that it was all real. I couldn't dismiss the thought that one day everything would explode in my face and I'd feel stupid for believing Simon--believing what he had told me, what he had taught me, and even that he existed at all.

"I often ask myself the very same questions," Simon said, after a long moment of thought. It was his turn at the register. The redheaded cashier rang up his purchase and Simon handed over the money.

"And what do you come up with for an answer?" I asked, as the cashier gave Simon his change. He picked up his bag of sweets off the counter and together we walked around the candy store while I decided what I'd buy.

"You're my answer. So what if it's all my own invention? Did our meetings help you? Did they improve your situation? If so, does it even matter what's real and what isn't? Who cares if someone else might say that I'm talking nonsense? Do you remember that I taught you that there is no good or bad, that everything is just a point of view?"

"Of course," I said, and selected a cinnamon lollipop from a shelf.

"The same thing holds true as to whether something actually exists or not, whether something that we experience is real or imagined. There are only two truly relevant questions in life, they're: 'What's your path?' and 'Are you walking it?' Other questions don't really matter."

I took a small bite from the lollipop in my hand. "It sounds right to me. I guess it doesn't really matter if what you said is real or not. The change you helped me to make is what matters."

He was right. Just the other day, I thought about how the less importance I placed on getting a new belt, the more attainable it seemed. Of course I still wanted it. I never gave up on that. But it was no longer a goal that must be achieved. Like Mr. Miyagi said in the movie *The Karate Kid*, "In Okinawa, belt means no need rope to hold up pants." Dad always used to say, "Whoever has respect, doesn't need respect." I finally understood what he meant. My ability was internal and didn't require external recognition to highlight its existence.

Dad also said, "You need to work hard to gain respect." What if he was right? Maybe life is hard work indeed. Perhaps the belt *is* more important than the path. Maybe I'm just deluding myself into thinking that life would be a breeze if only I were an artist. Maybe this whole artist thing is just an illusion. Maybe I'm supposed to work hard like my parents. Maybe I'm not really an artist.

I don't know what happened to me, but Doubty and Perfecto joined forces and tried to overpower me. It was a struggle for them, one of many, to gain back the control they had once held over my mind. I forgave them for trying. After all they were just performing their role, while my role was to resist their influence and not let them win.

Simon must have sensed what was going on and decided to help me out. "What would you think if I told you that you were chosen to come down to this world to teach Kung Fu like your Master? And you're now in training to reach that goal, and this is all part of the process?" There he was, saying weird stuff again.

I looked at him, suspicious. "It sounds like something you just made up. Where are you going with this?"

"But could it be true?"

"I guess, but could it also not be true? What if everything in life is random? What if I failed the test because of some bad karma I was born with, or because the coach was random in his decisions that day?" I challenged Simon as much as I could to deepen my understanding of his viewpoint.

"Those possibilities might be true as well. I just want you to consider how you'd prefer to live your life. Would you rather be a Kung Fu artist who prepares himself to be a master, or would you rather be a forlorn character, like the figures in the Greek tragedies you learn about in school? They're just like toys in the hands of the violent, arbitrary gods who, just for their own amusement, punish humans with immutable karma, throwing trouble and disaster in their way for the sake of twisted entertainment."

I had already chosen, but I wanted to be sure before we went our different ways. Maybe my faith had weakened; maybe I feared that I couldn't manage to be an artist without Simon's help. I guess such emotions are part of an artist's path as well. "Everything you've just said makes sense to me. But suppose the world is random after all; isn't making a choice to see it your way really lying to myself? Is it like inventing a theory to avoid facing reality?"

"If you're in Tel Aviv and you tell yourself that you're in New York, then you're lying to yourself," he said. "The city where you are isn't a relative thing. But your reality is relative. The way you look at and interpret your life, creates your experience. What you experience is what matters. Your interpretations keep changing."

"What do ya--- ouch!" I screamed. Someone pushed me from behind. I turned around, fists clenched, my face blazing with anger.

"What's up Ehud?" Kid asked me, startled, but still wearing a big smile. "You don't say hello anymore?"

Immediately, my fists relaxed and the red left my face. "Hey Kid, what's up? Sorry I didn't see you, buddy. What are you doing here?"

"What do you think?" He said, and waived a package of chocolate covered almonds at me.

"Oh, yeah," I chuckled. "Where did you get those? They're my favorite."

"Check out aisle two," he said. "Need to run now. Catch up with ya later."

I turned to Simon and tried to remember what we'd been saying before Kid interrupted. "Where were we?"

"I was just about to show you how your experience changes when your interpretation changes, then you got your own example."

I raised an eyebrow. "What do you mean?"

"When this kid pushed you, you were ready to fight. You experienced his push as an attack, but when you turned around and saw that it was your friend, your whole experience changed. The fact that he pushed you didn't change, just your interpretation."

"But he didn't mean to attack me."

"That's right, but usually you don't know what the other side meant to do."

"Hmmm, I guess. Do you have another example?"

"At times, you might perceive your mother as heartless since, instead of letting you play outside, she makes you stay inside to do homework. In the future, you may thank her for the actions which contributed to the person you'll grow up to be. You might even tell everyone that, thanks to your mother who insisted that you complete your homework, it has become easy for you to learn and succeed. Your interpretation of her actions will change. Viewpoint is relative."

I looked out of the storefront window into the street and watched the people entering the office building on the other side of the street. Then I walked to the other side of the store and watched the street again. From there I couldn't see the entrance to the building. I could see how changing my point of view, changed what I saw. "But what's the benefit in changing my viewpoint?" I asked.

"Have you ever dreamed of living in paradise?" He pointed his hands toward the shelves of candy, our candy heaven. "It's easy to move there. You just have to decide that you're there. If you change your perspective, all of the negativity, the hell in your life will lose its impact. Hell is just another view point. It's a place where there's no heaven, like darkness is where there's no light. Change your point of view. Let light into your life by opening your heart, and shadows will disappear. Deliberately create the reality that you choose. Flow, don't drift."

It was apparent that I still had much to discover. But, unlike before, being reminded that I had a lot to learn didn't stress me out. It's all part of the process and the process is blessed.

"I want you to remember three important things that will help you throughout life." Simon raised one finger. "First, don't believe a word of what I've told you from our first meeting until now. You may adopt any bit of my theories which make sense, anything that suits you or makes you happy, but don't accept something just because I said it."

He raised another finger. "Secondly, don't believe anybody. Each one of us sees the world limited by his own perception. Before embracing someone else's words, check to see if those words really fit you."

He showed me three fingers. "Finally, don't even believe yourself. The majority of the beliefs you hold weren't adopted deliberately. You picked them up by hearing someone else say what they believe, then you added them to your 'belief inventory' without properly examining them."

"What do you mean?" I asked.

"For example, the belief that you aren't good enough, which was one of the causes for your failure at the belt test; I'm sure that you didn't consciously come up with that. When you pinpoint a belief you have, ask yourself, 'How does this belief make me act? Would I rather act differently?' Perhaps a particular belief system suited you in the past but it doesn't suit you anymore. If that's the case, drop it. Review your beliefs every day, if they aren't relevant, replace them with new beliefs. Use your belief system to create the future you want, and not the one that others impose on you."

"Wait a second," I put down the box of caramels I had been holding. "If I stop believing everyone else, does that mean I'll need to learn everything all on my own? Isn't it better to learn from others who have more experience? Mom always says, 'why reinvent the wheel?'"

"Great question." His eyes shone. "Why reinvent the wheel? Maybe it's more fun to be the explorer who discovers the world and experiments with new things, instead of living in a boring world, where everything has already been discovered."

"Interesting answer," I said.

"Why reinvent the wheel?" he asked, again. "Maybe if you try, you'll create a new and better wheel, one that hasn't yet been invented."

"Hmmm... anything else?" I asked, half-jokingly.

"Why reinvent the wheel? Why not?"

"Seriously!"

"Why reinvent the wheel? Because you can!"

"That's it?"

"Why reinvent the wheel? No, why, really?"

"And what's the right answer?"

"All of the above, of course. Experience different perspectives, then you'll reach beyond your limits and expand your capabilities. Examine the wheel that someone else has already invented. See if it fits you or not. There is no one right way to be an artist. Part of being an artist is finding the path that is right for you."

"Thanks. I'm willing to add that concept into my belief system," I said. "I will pay attention so I can learn to adopt beliefs that contribute to my success, and drop any belief that doesn't." I wanted to show him that I understood.

"And how do you define success?" He asked, while opening up his bag and pulling out a piece of marzipan. He offered me one, I took a bite and it was delicious.

"Oh... What do you mean? Success is when... you're successful, right?"

"Success is relative, too. Everybody has their own definition of success. People consider others successful if they excel at sports, get good grades, become famous, or make a lot of money. Your mom might see her children's education as her greatest success. Your own definition of success is something you should explore. What does it really mean to you? Maybe the way that you define it is borrowed from someone else, and no longer suits you. Ask yourself: what is success for me? Is my definition appropriate for the path I walk?"

I smiled. Even success was relative, who would have thought? Six months ago, for me, success was getting the Green Belt. My perspective had changed and for me, today, being successful meant being an artist. I no longer equated winning any belt with success. In the future, success might mean being a dojo master. Sure, I could see how the definition of success could change.

"Can something that looks like a failure actually be a success?" I asked. "I mean, from another point of view?"

"Totally. There's a famous story about Thomas Edison. After a few hundred unsuccessful attempts to invent an electric light bulb, a New York Times reporter asked him, 'How does it feel to have failed several hundred times?' You know what he said?"

"No. If I were him I'd have given up after two or three attempts and left the world in the dark."

"He said, 'I haven't failed hundreds of times. I haven't failed once. I have succeeded in proving that those few hundred ways won't work. When I've eliminated the ways that won't work, I'll find the way that will work.' Several thousand more of these kinds of successes followed. Eventually, Edison found a way that worked and he invented the electric light bulb. He experienced a different reality. For him every failure was just another step toward achieving his goal. He knew that failure is an attitude, not an outcome, and without attempting, no one can get results."

"Wow," I said.

"Failure is also relative. For one person, failure is an attempt that didn't produce the desired results, for another person, failure is being anything other than number one."

"And what's a failure for you?" I asked.

"I used to define failure as giving up. As long as I kept trying and walking toward my goal, like Edison, I didn't fail. Recently I've changed my definition. Now, if I haven't learned a lesson, I've failed. As long as I've learned something, anything, from an attempt at accomplishing a goal, it's not a failure, but a successful lesson."

"Got it. I think May also knows that. When we play ball, she's rarely able to steal the ball from me, yet she never gives up or tells herself that she has failed. Just like Edison, she'll keep trying until she succeeds. Failure is not an option for her. An unsuccessful attempt is just another joyful step on her path."

"Great example." He smiled. "What are you looking at?"

"I think the chocolate I want was supposed to be here. There's none left."

"Is that why you look sad? I thought something really bad happened."

"You don't understand," I said, "It's Alisa's favorite, and mine, too."

"And what if you look at it differently?"

"How?"

"I don't know," he said, "I thought maybe you can find another way to look at it."

I closed my eyes and connected to *feel*. "Hmmm, let me see. I do have a bag full of other candies, so I guess I should be happy, but I want this one too."

"So?"

"I think I'll ask one of the employees here if they have more in the back, and if not, I'll ask when they are going to get a new delivery. I'm always happy to come here."

"Sounds like a plan."

"Look!" I said pointing up. "There is a different brand of chocolate covered almonds. Maybe I should try those, what do you think?" I looked at him and he flashed me a smile. I smirked, and took down a box. "Damn, I hate it when you're right. I feel happier now. This is exactly what you were trying to show me, right?"

Simon didn't answer; he just rolled his eyes and then winked.

"So how come most people can't see your path?" I asked. "I mean, how come people see such a different reality then yours? They see a reality where there's absolute good and evil, total right and total wrong. The path isn't important to them, but the goal is everything and controls everything. What we just discussed would sound like complete craziness to them." I felt Doubty sneaking up, about to challenge my insights with the oldest trick in his book. "But, is it possible that everyone else is wrong and I'm right?"

"Have you ever seen a tree grow?"

Sometimes I thought he had prepared a list of strange questions to counter every question I had. "Yes. Years ago when Grandpa was still alive, we planted a small tree together in his backyard. Every time I came to visit, I saw that it had grown new branches. After a while, it grew to be a tall tree, taller than me, and even taller than Grandpa."

"What caused the tree to grow?"

I got a little sad thinking of Grandpa. "Either Grandpa or I watered it twice a week with the garden hose that was attached to the rusty faucet in the courtyard."

"Did you water the branches?"

"Of course not." I rolled my eyes. "We watered the soil around the tree. As usual, I don't understand where you're going with this."

"But if the branches were the ones to grow, why would you water the soil around the tree?" he asked.

"What's up with you today? We watered the ground around the tree. The water seeped through the dirt to the tree's roots. The roots drank from below and the tree grew up."

"And how do you know there were roots? Could you see them?" he paused. "It's simple when you use the example of a tree. Every kid knows that you water the soil, the water seeps down to the roots, the roots drink and the tree grows. The process is simple and clear."

"That's right, just like I said."

I got in line to pay for everything I had picked, and Simon stood beside me. "But with the tree of life, you can't see it. Say someone hurts you, but you don't know why. The roots, which are the reasons behind the hurtful act, are hidden. You only see the branches, which are the hurtful results."

"What exactly do you mean?" I asked, although I thought I understood.

"Life is divided into two parts. The first part is what we see, the results and events experienced in everyday life, like branches of a tree. The second part is what is hidden, the reasons behind the events and the causes of the results; they're the roots which you aren't aware of. Can you think of an example from one of our meetings?" he asked, letting me find the answer myself.

I looked down sadly, biting my upper lip. "Yes. It's just like what happened to me with Tom and Rafael. I only saw their bullying. That's what was visible. I missed their home situation, their pain, and how Tom wishes his family life were more like mine, more stable. I missed that Rafael protects Tom like I defend Alisa. I missed how cruel their Dad is..."

I paused, remembering the first day I met Simon. I had just failed the belt test and I blamed the whole world for it. Eventually I learned that both my attitude and lack of preparation were the real causes for my failure. "You're right," I said. "Most people are too lazy to dig and discover the hidden roots. They aren't even aware that these roots exist or, if they are, they prefer to ignore their existence. They see only the branches and therefore, to them, the branches are all that matter. It's almost like what they can't see, doesn't exist. Out of sight, out of mind."

Simon nodded. "Some people may even try to fight the branches and stop their growth, other people may try to pull on the branches to make them grow faster. They don't get that what feeds the roots underground is what makes the branches grow above. If you water a tree, it grows. If you also add plant food and fertilizer to the soil, it'll grow even faster and stronger. If you poison the soil, the tree will get sick or die. Just like with humans. We, as opposed to trees, feed ourselves not only with food, but with thoughts and emotions. These things can nourish our spirit and we can shine, or they can infect our being and we can suffer."

I was happy that I had learned to dig deeper, and therefore could be more aware. Edison found more than a thousand ways that didn't work, until he eventually found the way he had been searching for all along. Not everyone can be Edison, but that is no reason to ignore the roots. Doubty tried to poison my roots. My roots weren't going to allow this, so he was about to lose this round. As I expected, Doubty fled my mind in a panic. He couldn't cope with such insights.

"Do you want your candy in a bag or in a box?" A bored cashier asked, interrupting my train of thought. It was my turn at the register. Simon waved farewell and left.

27 - THERE ARE ONLY TWO MASTERS IN THE ENTIRE WORLD WHO CAN HELP ME

My last encounter with Simon was at our park bench several hours before the Green Belt test. It was a sunny day, but the minute I arrived, it started to rain. The rain was warm, and big soft drops of water splashed my face. A few parents quickly herded their kids off the playground. The kids protested, but they were forced to join their parents under the cover of a nearby kiosk.

"This is my favorite weather," I said. I raised my palms to the sky and opened my mouth, catching drops on my tongue. "Perfect for our last lesson. Look what a beautiful rainbow," I said, pointing my finger at the sky.

Simon sneezed twice. I too, never sneeze once.

"Bless you. What else do I need to know to excel at the test?"

"You already have all the knowledge you need," he said. "However, I'll give you some last words of wisdom and inspiration." He paused for a long second and then swallowed hard before continuing. "I want you to know that I love you, you'll always be with me, and I'll always be with you!"

"What do ya mean by that?" My eyebrows lifted. "Love me? Always be with me? Aren't you an old Tiberiaser who lives in a retirement home, that just maybe I'll never see again? Or maybe you're just a creation of my imagination that serves to prepare me for the coming test. Sort of like the genie that lives under Alisa's bed and guards her from bad dreams."

"I wish it was that easy to explain who I am," he sighed. "During our first meeting I presented myself in a way that suited the moment. You weren't yet ready to know my real identity. But now it's time to tell you the whole story." He paused to take a deep breath, studying my face.

I sat down heavily on the bench. Two cats on the other side of the trail stopped fighting over which of them would hide under a board that would cover them from the rain, to watch us. *Maybe they want to hear Simon's confession as well*, I thought. "I'm listening."

Simon took off his big sunglasses and the light coming from his eyes blinded me for a second. I shaded my eyes with my hand until I felt it safe to look at him again. When I put my hand down, Simon was gone.

"Who are you? Where's Simon," I asked the stranger standing in front of me.

"Take a good look at me."

I studied his face for a moment until I could see that this stranger had my eyes and nose, but he also looked like a thinner, younger, beardless version of Simon.

"Are you related to Simon?" I asked.

He put his hands on my shoulders. "Give me a few minutes and I'll explain everything to you. I want to tell you Simon's full story, okay?"

"But where is he?"

One of Simon's smiles covered this man's face. "Don't worry. I'll explain and you'll soon understand everything. Is that alright?"

I wasn't sure what to say, but it was time for answers and this guy seemed to have them. "Okay, go ahead," I said, quietly.

"Thanks. When I was a young boy, I went to see Bruce Lee at the movies in the old neighborhood theatre. I sat with all my friends on the wooden chairs, mesmerized by the action on the screen. I wanted to be a Kung Fu artist just like him. On my way home from every movie, I'd imitate his moves from the film, fighting imaginary enemies, and always winning."

"Yes, I do that too," I said, and chuckled. "Wait a second, so you're a Kung Fu artist? Why---"

He used his most reassuring tone. "Ehud, please be patient, I promise that by the end of my story you'll see what it is that I see. It took me a whole year to convince my mom to sign me up for a Kung Fu class. I had asked, begged, nagged, threatened, and bargained, until finally she agreed, under the condition that I get good grades. This mission wasn't a problem for me, and soon I started to practice. During the first week of training, a new dream was born. I wanted to be a Kung Fu master and teach others. In my mind, I'd be the owner of a dojo in some poor neighborhood and train young children on the Kung Fu path. They'd come to my dojo instead of wandering around the streets and hanging out with gangs. In this fantasy, I'd be the hero of the neighborhood. However, the dream was shattered when I failed my Green Belt test and quit the training."

"Wow, that's just what happened to me." I said, and swallowed against the lump in my throat.

He licked his upper lip with his tongue, like I do when I have something important to say. "Yes, we do have a similar story. For years I forgot the dream to be a master, and went on with my life. The usual kinds of things happened to me. I didn't take too many risks and didn't experience much disappointment. Every so often a new dream would pop up. I'd try to make this new dream a reality, but when things got rough I'd lose interest and give up, like I gave up on the Green Belt."

"Yeah, I almost gave up too," I said.

"Right. My thirtieth birthday was the happiest day of my life. My friends decided to make me a king for one day. Actually it was for a long weekend. They 'kidnapped' me on Thursday from work and took me on a flight to the north. They spoiled me the whole weekend. I especially loved rafting on the Jordan River and swimming in the hexagonal, natural pool, surrounded by basalt rocks. We spent a whole day in the most amazing spa that had a view of the Sea of Galilee. And the meals? Just thinking about the restaurants we visited makes me rub my belly with pleasure. I was on top of the world."

I licked my lips. "Boy! Sounds amazing."

Now the rain showers stopped, and joyful kids began running toward the muddy playground.

"Yes," he said, "but when I returned home at the end of the weekend I felt so lonely. It was late, and I had to get some sleep because the next day I had an early meeting at the office. All of a sudden I felt that I was wasting my life. Between a steady diet of hard work, and some small troubles I encountered from time to time, there wasn't much joy in my life. I had just experienced a high peak, maybe the highest I'd ever have. I was king for a weekend, but now what was left?"

"According to Mom, something similar happened to my dad. She called it a midlife crisis."

He laughed heartily and punched my arm playfully. "My father always said, 'In life, only one thing is certain - death.' So on this night, I was thinking that all that's left was just to grow old quietly, wait for death, and hope not to suffer too much until it comes. Even my father, who used to symbolize power and strength for me, was now aging. He had been spending so much of his time with the new friends he made in the waiting rooms at various doctor's offices. I wondered, *Is this what's in store for me? Is this the future?*"

I shook my head. "Wow, sounds like the end isn't going to be good."

He grinned. "Wait and see. Instead of going to bed, I heavily clomped up the stairs of my twenty-floor building, feeling inside like I was a hundred years old. Finally I dragged myself up onto the roof. I looked out at the landscape of Tel Aviv, spread below at my feet. In the darkness, I couldn't see the parks, the sea or the outlines of anything human. I just saw an unorganized mixture of cold and alienated towers, pushing against the sky. My position on the roof represented my life. I had climbed as high as possible. I was young, healthy, and had a great job; all that was left was old age, sickness and death. From where I stood, there was no place to go but down. I felt depressed."

I reached for him. "I hope you're not going to jump. Actually, you made it here, so I guess I don't have to worry." I settled back onto the bench, listening.

"That's right, I didn't jump. I lay down on the roof facing the sky. The coldness of the roof reached my back through my thin shirt. I closed my eyes. The night felt icy and dark, like my future. My despair grew by the minute. When I opened my eyes they were filled with tears. It was the first time I had cried in over twenty years."

"I'd like to be able to cry, too," I said, sadly.

"One day you will," he said and smiled sympathetically. "At that moment, I experienced a mix of despair and joy. I was happy about the liberation of finally being able to cry. Those tears had been trapped within me for many years, just waiting for the moment of release. Every tear captured a difficult emotion. Now, the tears joyfully spilled forth from my eyes, rolling down my cheeks with their salty warmth, flushing the negative emotions out of me."

A bitter taste filled my throat. I glanced at the trail and watched two kids passing by with ice cream cones in their hands. I bet if I had an ice cream, it would taste bitter. "I envy you right now," I said, softly. "Sorry, go on."

"Suddenly, behind my tears," he continued, "I noticed something glimmering. I rubbed my eyes, drying the tears. I looked up and saw endless stars high in the sky, bright and shiny. I screamed with joy, 'YES,' and jumped into the air reaching my hands up high, trying to catch some stars.

At that moment, everything became clear to me. That rooftop wasn't the top of the world, and I hadn't reached my peak in life. The roof was low, close to the ground; it had only appeared high from that point of view. This was parallel to my life, I just needed to look at myself from another perspective. I hadn't peaked, in fact, I probably hadn't yet even begun to rise. There were a million ways for me to grow more and to reach further than I had so far. I could reach all the way to the stars. If I didn't see a way to rise higher or progress, it only meant that I... didn't yet see *how* to do it."

I was relieved. "Yes! Good ending."

He grinned. "My tale isn't over yet. I ran back to my apartment, jumping down a few steps at a time. I went straight to bed. I was both exhausted and excited. I fell into the most pleasant sleep I'd had in years. Just before I woke up I had a dream. I was in a race. A gun fired to signal the start of the race and I tried to run with everyone, but I was frozen in place. I struggled to move but nothing happened.

"*Concentrate*! I heard a voice behind me. I turned my head back and couldn't believe my eyes. Bruce Lee was standing there talking to me in English. His voice was out of sync with his lip movements, like in the old Kung Fu movies dubbed from Chinese. *Focus, man*, he said. I tried to focus more on the track ahead of me. Bang! I was freed from the invisible chains that held me. I started sprinting down the track like I was strapped to a Boeing jet engine.

"My alarm screeched loudly: *Rise and shine, sleeping beauty,* making me tumble out of my dream. When I originally recorded this alarm message to my cell, I thought it was the coolest thing, but over time it had become quite annoying. That morning however, it sounded like angels singing. I jumped out of bed, a huge smile covering my face. I called my office and asked them to reschedule all of my meetings."

"It's a nice story," I interrupted. "But I still don't know who you are and what happened to Simon."

He chuckled. "You're cute. We're almost there. Okay?"

"I guess."

"Well, I *Googled* local Kung Fu dojos and couldn't believe my luck when I saw that my old dojo was still active. I wasted no time, got dressed and headed down to the dojo. It was just the way I remembered it. I almost cried again out of excitement, when I saw the mats and the familiar pictures on the walls. I registered myself for a class, and that very evening, I began my Kung Fu practice again as a white belter. After class, I rushed up the stairs to my building's rooftop and announced to the whole world that I'd be a Kung Fu Master!"

He stopped his story to kick an escaped ball back to a group of teenagers. They thanked him and he continued. "My training advanced at a fast and steady pace. I practiced for two hours, twice a week after work; one hour of Kung Fu and then one hour of Tai Chi. Two forms of martial arts that complement each other, one active and one passive. This time I walked the artist path during my training. It made the entire process easier and my improvement was fast. Adults don't advance in belts as quickly as children, but I didn't care since the path was more important. Don't get me wrong, the goal was significant too, but it was just secondary to my real objective."

"Wow! Exactly like I experienced it."

"You bet. Everything was going well, but then one day I started feeling restless, like a fighter. I was resisting something but I wasn't sure what. One evening, after Tai Chi, I went up to my roof to think. I sat under my friends, the stars, and looked up at their shining bodies. The moon smiled at me, full and big, and the little stars looked like its children.

After a moment of reflection, it came to me. 'That's it! I got it!' I shouted aloud. I got my yellow belt about a year ago, and in less than six months I'd be tested for a Green Belt. I was afraid to fail again! I now knew that the path was a lot more important to me than the goal, but knowing isn't enough when fear takes over."

"How did it happen?" I asked. "If you were on the artist path, how did you slip from it into fear?"

"I asked myself the very same question. I realized that deep down inside me, crouched in a corner, there was a frightened thirteen-year-old child. He was already going through this story. He practiced, was tested, failed, and gave up his dream. He was worried that the story was going to repeat itself. The stars reminded me of him."

"So what did you do?"

"I knew of only two masters that could help me pass this test like an artist. The first one was you. I mean ---"

"Me?"

"Yes, you," he said. "My name is Ehud. I'm you in twenty years."

"How can you be me? It's impossible. Are you fooling around? And who's Simon? I don't get what you're saying at all. You lost me big time."

"You're the younger me, the thirteen-year-old me that already tried and failed. That's why I chose you as the first master. Only you have the ability to show me what to avoid if I want to succeed."

"Sorry, I still don't get it. And who's the second master? You said there were two, right?"

"Yes. The second master was born from a sentence I read in a magazine, 'Don't let who you are get in the way of who you could be.' This master is the older me. He's us many years from now. He has already been through it all. He not only won the Green Belt, but also the black belt and he trains others."

"I still don't get it," I protested. "How can I be a master if I'm a kid that knows nothing and doesn't exist anymore? And how can the other master teach you from the future? It sounds crazy, like the movie, *Back to the Future*."

"You're funny. I loved that movie, too. You're my inner child, the one who I repressed all of these years. Even though you aren't real anymore, your memories, fears, and deprivation are still very alive within me every day. I, you, will grow to be a master in the future based on my actions in the present. Even though the masterful us doesn't exist yet, today I decide what and who he's going to be. He's my goal. I've decided that he will be a Kung Fu master. You and he together are guiding me on my growth path."

"But if this other master and I are just in your head, how can we help you?"

"I invited the two of you to meet each other and talk in my head."

"How can we meet?" I asked.

"I realized that the best way to grow is to contemplate my present from opposite directions simultaneously. So I had to look at it from both the past and the future. The point of view of my past was you, my repressed inner child. And the point of view of my future was Simon, the more experienced adult me. This way, I could combine the experience of the past and the vision of the future to guide me through the present.

"Let's say for a second that I understand who I am," I said. "Who is the future?"

"It's Simon."

"He can't be, his name should be Ehud too. What am I missing?"

"Fair question," he said. "I know you too well. If I approached you as the older Ehud, the Kung Fu master, you wouldn't let it go. You'd expect the older version of us to tell you the future and teach you Kung Fu. At first, you even wanted the retired veterinarian to be your master. The only reason you dropped that idea is because of the image that I presented to you, because of the disguise. That's why I had to exhibit the older us as Simon.

"But there really is someone named Simon. I met him on a class trip to Tiberias when I was just a few months older than you are now. He sat on the beach fishing. I was so fascinated by his personality that I even skipped canoeing on the Jordan River with my classmates, just to sit next to him and listen to his stories. He had a million stories about the art of fishing, handling animals and his friends in the retirement home.

"He told me all about evil Alfred, who's actually his best friend, and beautiful Mary, who drove them both nuts for years. He also told me about his son and grandson, who lived in America. I knew that a Simon character would be the perfect disguise. I knew you'd feel comfortable talking to him because I already was, when I was your age.

"The Simon I created for you is full of contrasts because he's a reflection of me. Like me, he knows the artist path, but still doesn't fully create the reality he chooses to experience. I gave him the wisdom I want to adopt into my life. I gave him lightness and a mischievous nature. That's exactly how I want to be when I'm his age.

"The conversation in my head between you two, connected my past and the future – which I gave to you as Simon. You've both been training me for half a year, and tonight I'm going to get a Green Belt." The thirty-something-year-old Ehud finished his confession. The waves of excitement emanating from his body crashed into me like ocean waves breaking on the beach.

I began to digest all of the new information. After a moment of thought, I pounced on him with a million questions like I had when I first met Simon; only this time I wasn't sure his answers would be any better than mine. "So Simon and I are actually the masters? You, the middle aged Ehud, is our student? Does that mean that I'm not real?"

"That's right. While you thought that Simon was teaching you, I was really learning from your interactions. Your inquiries and his responses served as my lessons. Your questions encouraged me to look for deeper answers. The questions that Simon posed, which were supposedly helping you, actually drew out your perspective, so I could learn from it. Your questions that Simon labeled as 'great' were those that really made me think and consider something new. You reminded me how to be an artist. You reminded me that life is an art not a fight. The time you spent with Simon was the time where I feel I've grown the most in my life."

I can't believe what I'm hearing. He's actually my student. I'm his master, I thought. Then something occurred to me. "Wait, are you mad at me for failing you at the Green Belt test?" I asked, apprehensively. "You failed because of me. I mean, if I'd have passed the test and if I hadn't quit, maybe today you could've been a black belt instead of just a yellow one."

"Six months ago, when your meetings with Simon started, I'd answer: no. But from today's viewpoint I can tell you that I was angry then. I wasn't mad because you failed, but because you quit... because I quit. But I didn't admit that anger to even myself."

I looked into his eyes. "Were you really mad at me?"

"Yes, but the opportunity to hear you again reminded me what an amazing kid I was, and how I always did the best I could. That's why

I want you to know that I love you. By experiencing this love, I really can accept everything you've... I've... we've been through. I can see how it led to my growth, brought me to where I am today, and gave me direction for the future."

"So something good came out of it, right?"

"Indeed. Thanks to you, today the belt isn't my goal anymore. I still want it, and I will get it, but it's not the real goal. The purpose of art is art itself. Surrendering led to a victory, the path became the target. If you, I, hadn't given up as a kid, I could've probably fought my way to the Green Belt in the next round of testing. But this achievement wouldn't have brought more than a few minutes of happiness. Today I love you because, thanks to your crawling, I've learned to walk and now I'm ready to fly. I feel ready to train others to become artists too. Thank you, young Ehud!"

"You're welcome. I'm glad to help, even if it seemed to me that Simon was helping me," I said, quietly.

"One more thing," he continued, "the conversations we had brought me back to my elementary school days. I was both happy and sad to remember the Rafael and Tom of those days. Back then, I considered them absolute evil until we all became friends. Rafael grew up to be a platoon commander. Sadly, he died saving his friends when their base was attacked. It happened when Tom and I were still in high school. After Rafael's death, he received a certificate for his courage. Do you remember how evil we thought he was? How afraid we were of him? In that heroic moment only the enemy could perceive him as evil."

"That's so sad," I said, and swallowed hard so as not to cry. Even so, it would probably take another twenty years before I could cry. The tears would flow only when I become the adult Ehud lying in despair on the roof, gazing at the stars, before deciding to recommence Kung Fu training. "I've already realized that I was mistaken in the way that I judged them. What about Tom? What happens to him?"

"Tom and I were both members of the high school running team. We practiced together for hours every week and eventually became best friends. He spent more time at my home than his own. It was almost natural when he asked my permission to date Alisa. Of course, I said 'yes,' and soon after they became a couple.

I remember one particular double date. We went to an amusement park. Tom tossed three balls into a small hole about thirty feet away, winning a giant teddy bear for Alisa. My girlfriend asked him where he learned to aim like this. He grinned sadly and said, 'before my Dad went to prison, Rafael and I spent our nights in the streets to avoid getting beaten. While other kids were having dinner in their homes, we kind of hung out in the school yard.'"

"What did they do there?" I interrupted him, saddened by this information. "They probably had no one to play with."

"That's right. Tom said that their favorite game was hitting cans from a distance with small stones. That's how he learned to throw so accurately. I asked if they threw stones at cats, too. I remembered how angry I was at them for abusing cats. Tom stroked his dreadlocks for a few seconds, then answered in a broken voice: 'when dad would catch Rafael and beat him real hard, Rafael would run away full of rage. I'd run after him, keeping a safe distance so as not to accidentally get in the way. Rafael would usually go toward the school, sit on the fence outside, and throw small stones at the stray cats that got too close to the road. He didn't try to hurt them, only to scare them away from the passing cars.'"

"That sounds like a stupid thing to do. Why did he do it?"

"It was comforting to him, I guess. On the one hand, the action of throwing the stones was a release and on the other hand, his perception that he was saving the cats made him feel like he was worth something. He never felt that way when his dad was home. When Rafael progressed with his Kung Fu training, he no longer needed to release anger in that way so he stopped doing that. Tom told me that when he reminded Rafael of that, years later, Rafael was embarrassed about having thrown those stones."

"Now I'm embarrassed that I hated them," I said, sadly. "Rafael was a good guy."

"Yes. After Tom told me this story, he closed his eyes and whispered, 'Rafael had a golden heart. He always protected me and never hurt me. You can't believe how much he suffered in his short life and how many beatings he took to protect me and Mom.'"

The lump in my throat returned. "Simon... I mean, Ehud, I have another question," I whispered. "If I understand you correctly, you're my future; which means I'll quit Kung Fu for the next twenty years. So this is all set and I can't change it. Right?"

He smiled, wiping his eyes at the end of his sleeve. "I'm just one possible future. Now that you know me, you can choose to create any future you want. You're an artist. Every second is an opportunity to create a new future, and you do this by making choices. You've already changed your future. You've started to practice and you'll be tested for the Green Belt in a couple of hours. And most importantly, we aren't going to separate again. I'll continue to carry you in me everywhere I go. However, from now on instead of being my frightened inner child, you'll be my artist inner child." He tightened the belt around the Kung Fu suit that he was wearing. His test was coming soon as well, and it was time for him to head out toward our dojo, to be tested in his own reality.

"Good luck with the test," I said. "Can I ask one last question?"

"Please." He smiled at me for the millionth time.

"How does my story end? Do I get the belt?"

"You already know." He beamed one last pleasant smile at me. "You don't need me to finish the story. You're also an artist, remember?"

"I understand." I smiled back. "Thanks for everything."

* * * * *

My name is Ehud, I'm thirty-three and a quarter years old, and I have a Green Belt in Kung Fu.

28 - WHAT? NO DINNER TONIGHT?

JJ looked at Gill. His big eyes were wide open, his gaze was peaceful and quiet. Sara remained seated. David stood up and walked to the dining table. He stroked his belly. "What? No dinner tonight?"

"Come on, Dad, let us digest the story for a moment. Didn't it make you think at all?"

David sat at the head of the table. "It's a good story and everything, but now I'm ready to digest the feast that your mom fixed for us. The smell of that roast has been driving me nuts for over an hour."

Sara went to JJ and gave him a big hug. "I loved the story," she said. Gill rose also. He planted an affectionate kiss on JJ's forehead before joining his father at the table. JJ and Sara went into the kitchen and began bringing the food out.

Once they had all had their fill of the roast, potatoes, bread, salads and dessert, David excused himself to lie on the couch in the living room. He turned on the TV. "JJ, I appreciate the story. Even though I can't agree with everything, I do feel somehow better. Anyhow, it's news time, so no more stories, alrighty?" he said, and loosened his belt with a sigh of satisfaction.

The remaining three slowly stepped into the back yard. "So Uncle JJ, you conned us, right? The whole story just happened in your head. It wasn't real," Gill said, quickly, to prevent his mom from starting a new conversation.

"Real is a relative concept, my dear Gill. You should know that by now. This story, or one similar to it, is told in the head of everyone who grows tired of fighting and opts instead for a more multi-dimensional artistic approach."

"Even though this artist path sounds a little weird," Gill said, "I already figured out how that story can help me with my problems. The Kung Fu in the story symbolizes life, and the belt symbolizes achievements and goals. The story explains how to win the belt, or achieve your goals, and that's exactly what I'm going to do."

JJ punched Gill's shoulder warmly. "I'm impressed with the way you analyzed the story, you should rock in literature class."

"I wish." Gill blushed. "But, if it works for me as well as it worked for Ehud, I'll owe you big time. I think that if I surrender to the impulses to do other things while I'm supposed to be learning, it will be easier for me to concentrate. I also need to remember that the path is more important than the goal."

JJ was pleased. "Well, well. I'm glad that you're adopting some ideas from the story."

"Don't you worry. From now on, I'll practice the artist path at every opportunity."

Sara rolled her eyes and chimed in. "I'm sorry JJ, but I'm somewhat less optimistic than my angel. In theory, the artist path sounds wonderful, but I've got a bit more life experience than Gill; I know the way of life is anything but easy."

"No one promised, sis, that the road would be easy. As an artist, the path is just different. If you aren't happy with your current state, why don't you try to change it?"

"I suppose I could," she answered pensively.

"As an adult, clearly you have more experience than a child," JJ said. "But sometimes less experience can be an advantage. A child isn't afraid to try new things. A child can succeed because he tries, where an adult already 'knows' that he's going to fail, so he may not even bother to try."

Sara frowned. "Maybe that's why it's easier for children to change their ways," she said, and looked off at the dark outline of houses against the sky. "I'm probably too old for that."

"Mom, you aren't *that* old," Gill quipped.

JJ put his hand on his sister's shoulder. "One big difference between an adult and a child is that the adult labels more things as impossible. However, just by walking the artist path, both child and adult can make the impossible, possible. It worked for me. Don't you think it's worth a try?"

JJ felt that he had already handled his own problems and returned to the artist path by recounting this story.

"Hey, don't get me wrong, JJ. I may be pessimistic by nature, but I'm going to try it anyway. I'm just not sure it will work."

"But it's worth a shot, right Mom? We'll practice together."

She hugged Gill and looked back at the house where her husband lay sprawled on the couch in front of the TV. "We're a family of fighters by nature, but I think maybe it's time we try a new way. I'll practice despite my fears that it won't work. I'll try to feel more compassion, the way Ehud did. I also want to try to create my own reality. It'd be great if I could create what I want."

Gill grinned. "Cool, Mom. I want to practice that as well."

"I suggest not trying, just doing," JJ said. "There's more believing in doing. I'm sure it will help you." He paused for a moment. "You may be surprised to hear, but this story helped me today, too. I needed it just as much as you. Although usually I can walk the artist path with my eyes closed, occasionally I stray from the road and need reminding."

"Really? I thought once you're an artist, you never want to go back," Gill said, with disbelief.

"You never *want* to go back," JJ grinned, "but sometimes the drama feels so real, that all you can see is the warrior path."

"Then you need to get back on track, right?"

"That's exactly what I just did," JJ confirmed. "Today, there were two important ideas that resonated the most for me. 'Every nothing is something else,' because that reminded me to transform cons, into pros. And 'Why fear falling if you can get up again?'"

"Yes, I loved those ideas, too," Sara said. "But what about Dave? It seems like your story didn't make any impression on him." She sounded disappointed.

"No worries," JJ said, "just give him some time. He needs to think about and absorb these ideas. It took me a few good years from when I first started learning about the artist path until I took the first big step on it. When the time is right, David will find his way. Each one of us has his own timing, pace, and direction."

Her eyes were sad. "I hope you're right."

"Mom, everything is gonna be fine. Dad ain't stupid, he knows what's good for him. Even if he has to crawl behind us on all fours down the artist path, he'll join us," Gill said, and burst out laughing.

JJ hugged them both. "You know, even if he doesn't change a thing, he's already on the path. Now that he heard all about the two paths, he has the ability to choose. This is being on the path. Think about it. It will answer many of the questions you might have."

EPILOGUE

During the following week, JJ kept reminding himself to walk on the artist path. He surrendered to his frustration and looked for ways to turn the nothing into something. He went over the details of his project again, and released the sense of helplessness that he had carried like a heavy cloud over his shoulders for some time. When doubts appeared, he sent Doubty packing, telling himself that there must be a solution. Once he felt like a wiz again, he *Googled* for other options to solve his chips problem. He had unsuccessfully searched before, but he knew that there had to be someone else who experienced a similar problem with *Easy Chips*.

It wasn't long before he found a forum of project managers that could prove useful. One of the members had experienced an identical problem with *Easy Chips*. The member posted a recommendation for a new provider that charged lower fees and could ship immediately. *Sometimes solutions can be so simple*, JJ thought. After he switched the provider, he'd give his employees the money he'd saved to encourage them to put in extra effort. Three weeks and a lot of long hours of work later, the project was back on schedule.

"I see that my magician returned from his little break," JJ's director complimented him at the executive meeting on Thursday. "You always manage to amaze me with your brilliant, yet simple solutions. It's like you create something out of nothing. One day you'll have to tell me your secret, huh? And do me a favor, don't ever let the wiz leave us again, alright?" He tapped JJ fondly on the shoulder. "By the way, I need you to pay a visit to a client in Paris this weekend. It requires a personal touch. Can you do this for me?" He presented the request as if he really needed JJ's help, but it was apparent that the trip was a reward for his good work.

* * * * *

Almost a month had passed before JJ and Sara's family got together again. JJ had been busy with his project and then had flown off for his week in Paris. The Friday of their next reunion, Sara and her family arrived earlier than usual. This time they seemed relaxed when they entered his home. After hugs and a few words of greeting, Sara headed to the kitchen while Gill went to change into his sports clothing.

"I have a new joke for you," David said to JJ. "The New York Knicks."

JJ sighed and put his hands on his hips. "I'm glad to see that you're in a better mood than the last time I saw you, but you should know that you can't destroy my good mood by bringing up the painful defeat of my team."

David took a seat on the couch. "Well, forget about it. It was only a game. You aren't going to believe what's happened since I last saw you."

"Aliens landed in your office and abducted Danny Cordova?"

David chuckled. "Well, to be honest, it's something much bigger, come see this picture."

JJ took David's cell phone and looked at the picture on the screen. "I see a pool, what's so special about it?"

"And in the pool, who do you see?"

"Someone swimming on her back."

"Come on JJ, don't you recognize the swimmer?"

JJ squinted at the screen. His jaw dropped. "Get out of here! You're not serious, is that Sara?"

"Yes. I couldn't believe it either. She started taking swimming lessons. She said she decided to surrender to her fear of water and approach the lessons as an artist, not as a fighter. So far, she's just been floating on her back or swimming with a life vest."

JJ took another look at the photo. "What do you mean 'just'? Getting her to wet her knees used to be a challenge."

"I know," David said. "She has taken six lessons so far. I think there might be something more to your story than what I noticed at first. Maybe I should try one of your tricks. Sara said I should start by being compassionate at work. Who knows. Maybe she's right."

"Maybe. If you don't try, you'll never know."

"I know, but believe me JJ, after what my office did to me, they deserve no compassion, forgiveness or mercy."

"Look, first of all, like Simon said, compassion and mercy aren't the same thing. Secondly, even if they don't deserve compassion, you have to remember that compassion is for your own good. It will help you to let go of your anger. The compassion isn't for their benefit. I'm sure they don't care if you feel compassion for them or not."

"I understand what you are saying, but the process is difficult. I'll take the time to think about it. In any event ---"

"Did he tell you about the swimming lessons?" Sara's head peeked out from the kitchen. "Isn't it amazing?"

JJ felt thrilled. "You're what's amazing, Sara. I'm impressed."

"Whenever I get frustrated that I can't swim yet, I remind myself that the path is more important than the goal and I need to enjoy it. It releases the stress. In the worst case scenario, there's always another summer."

"This is---" JJ started to say, but Sara interrupted him.

"And last week, Dave was late for dinner again. He promised to be home at 6:00, but then called to say that he was running late and would be home at 8:00. Gill was at basketball practice and dinner was ready. I'd lie if I said I didn't get upset. I was ready to call you and complain, but then I remembered your story. So, I looked for the something in that nothing; it was a great opportunity to catch up on some TV shows I had missed. It saved me from an unnecessary fight with Dave. Before I heard your story, I would've felt that it was my right to be furious, and I'd have labeled him as bad. But thanks to your story, I know that an artist can choose not to get upset. Besides it wasn't Dave's fault if he had to work late."

"I'm so happy to hear that." JJ paused. "Anything else?"

"Uh-huh, but, we.... you know, not everything is perfect. Just the other day, I got really upset in the mall when a bunch of kids shoved around an older guy and shouted curse words at him. I felt like I could kill them with my bare hands. They pulled out my warrior without even trying."

JJ put his hands on her shoulder. "Things like this happen all the time."

"What was I supposed to do?"

"There's no easy answer. I can just promise you that if you think, feel and act like an artist, you can find your own answers and maintain your inner peace."

"Right, like in your story. I know I still have a long way to go to become less of a warrior."

JJ winked. "Sure, just don't forget to enjoy getting there."

Sara sighed. "I will. Oh, one last thing, Gill passed a literature test for the first time this year. He got a nice, optimistic "C+." I bet he'll tell you all about it during game."

JJ smiled. "I'm sure."

"Yo, Uncle JJ." Gill burst into the room. Seeing JJ's smile beaming proudly at him, Gill frowned. "I guess she couldn't resist the temptation to tell you and ruined my surprise." He paused and took a deep breath. "Never mind. What's important is that I passed the test. Studying for the test was actually not so bad when I surrendered. Every time I wanted to quit studying, I tried to fully experience wanting to quit. I amplified the feeling of quitting to its edges until it was gone. I still need to practice more and improve. Now come on,

I'm going to rip your ass in basketball. Today you'll learn that basketball is an art, not a war."

Sara smiled and headed toward the yard door so she could watch a bit of the game. Gill jabbed a friendly elbow into JJ's ribs as he walked past him. "I also have some news about Michelle. You're gonna be proud of me. Guess who has a date tomorrow?" he whispered, so his parents wouldn't hear.

Gill ran outside. As JJ passed by Sara on his way outside, she took his hand. "I think you should write your story in a book. There's a whole world out there full of warriors just waiting for help to find their own inner peace path."

"Are you nuts?" JJ asked, dismissively. "I'm not a writer, what do I know about writing books? In any case, I have no time to sit down and write. Besides, what are the chances it would be published or that anyone would actually want to read it? And ---"

"JJ..."

- The End -

ABOUT THE AUTHOR

Joey Avniel is passionate about helping people to find their own inner peace. As a former officer in the army he mastered the way of the warrior, but was missing the essential components of peace and happiness. After his service he started to search his own path to inner peace. He received self-improvement training, and then trained others through several different self-improvement programs. Eventually he developed what he calls "The Artist Path," a path that guides anyone, even a warrior to find his own inner peace.
Joey's training includes energetic healing, self empowerment teaching, and first aid for suicidal people. Today he's an author and a speaker on the subject of inner peace. He is the co-founder of the publishing house – Barefoot Mind Inspiration and the co-creator of the website – www.mysuicidalthoughts.com – which helps people deal with and overcome suicidal thoughts.

Connect with the author online:

Blog: http://www.oneleggedseagull.com
Facebook: http://www.facebook.com/JoeyAvniel
Twitter: http://twitter.com/joeyavniel

www.ingramcontent.com/pod-product-compliance
Lightning Source LLC
LaVergne TN
LVHW051829080426
835512LV00018B/2793